"An engaging and illuminating read!"
-TY GIBSON

THE DEATH AND REBIRTH OF THE

INVESTIGATIVE
JUDGEMENT

MARCOS D. TORRES

Testimonials

" Marcos Torres has done us an excellent theological favor by revisiting the doctrine of the investigative judgment from the angle of its practical usefulness. Why believe anything, if it doesn't matter? Well, as it turns out, this dusty old doctrine matters immensely. The Death and Rebirth of the Investigative Judgment is both an engaging and illuminating read."

—— Ty Gibson, *Author/ Pastor*

" Marcos' insights on the Investigative Judgment breathe new life into what has become for so many an irrelevant and antiquated teaching from Adventism's humble beginnings. If the Investigative Judgment is to have any significance for the next generation of Adventism, Marcos' volume will be a key factor in its rebirth and rediscovery in a postmodern society."

—— Ingram London, *The Compass Magazine*

" Though I have not read all that Marcos has written on the Investigative Judgment, I have been intrigued by what I have. It's exciting to see a new generation taking up the mantle and seeking to make this crucial doctrine relevant for our church. Whether or not you would agree with everything, his writing is definitely worth reading."

——— Clifford Goldstein, *Sabbath School Editor*

" Pastor Marcos is on the cutting edge of ministry to people who have no religious or Christian background. His re-framing and repackaging of Adventist truth is insightful and exciting! You won't view the Pre-Advent Investigative Judgment as irrelevant, nerdy theology ever again!"

——— Tony Brandon, *Pastor*

" If you have ever struggled to see how the doctrine of the Investigative Judgment makes any meaningful difference in your life (let alone in the life of a secular person), this book will give you a fresh perspective. Marcos Torres' concept of reframing could help us present many of our cherished doctrines in a way that captures the attention of today's world."

——— Rachel Cobos, *Writer/Editor*

" Torres' exchanges a fear-based reading of the judgment for a love-based interpretation and, with depth of thought, captures in a compelling way our calling to be agents of change in the world. His book is a fresh, engaging, and Gospel-centered perspective that inspires the reader to participate in the reversal of suffering and the pragmatic vindication of God's character."

—— Adelina Alexe, *Writer/ Editor*

Acknowledgements

I would like to thank Ingram London and *The Compass Magazine* for supporting me in this project.

Contents

" In every age there is a new development of truth, a message of God to the people of that generation. The old truths are all essential; new truth is not independent of the old, but an unfolding of it. It is only as the old truths are understood that we can comprehend the new... It is the light which shines in the fresh unfolding of truth that glorifies the old. He who rejects or neglects the new does not really possess the old. For him it loses its vital power and becomes but a lifeless form.

—— Ellen G. White, *Lift Him Up, p. 306.*

Introduction

Outside of the first two – arguably three – generations of Adventists, many have found it difficult to explain and defend the Adventist doctrine of the Investigative Judgment. Today, it appears all robust discussion on the topic is relegated to the theological nerds among us – those who actually have the time and interest in dissecting matters of thought that the general population considers irrelevant and tedious. Therefore, we now have two problems before us: the mechanical issues related to the doctrine (exegesis, systematics, etc.) and the existential ones. In this book, it is the existential that I aim to contend with.

When dealing with the existential, the primary question before us is "why does it matter?" Life is, after all, a passing vapor. There is little in terms of time and resources, energy and opportunity, from which every being must construct some sort of effectual and meaningful life. To put my finite time toward the study of a doctrine which – even if mechanically demonstrable – has no real meaning is a tragic mismanagement of my finitude. And this is something no intelligent and self-aware being wants to do.

And it is this existential vacuum within the doctrine of the Pre-Advent Investigative Judgment that I believe is at the core of its demise despite our impressive capacity to mine from the text details, data, propositions and mechanics through which its accuracy can be endlessly defended. Because at the end of the day, life is absurd and difficult, filled with suffering and struggle which bombards our psyches from every conceivable angle, almost as if to strangle any will to life from within us. And if I am to believe anything it must be something capable of bringing order from that chaos and meaning from the mockery of an existence replete with anxieties and disappointments. To this end, I ask again – why does the Investigative Judgment truly matter? You may teach me its mechanics on Sabbath evening, but of what use is it on the proverbial Monday morning, filled with angst and traffic, rush and worry?

This book then, is a series of articles I wrote in an attempt to begin journeying for a solution to this existential question. It is not perfect and neither do I claim to have it all resolved. In fact, as you read this current book, I am in the process of authoring an entire book on the book of Daniel. So, this is only the beginning. However, given the feedback I have experienced thus far with the ideas and perspectives outlined here, I thought it worth the effort to make these articles more readily available, in one format, for easy reading.

I invite you therefore, to read, ponder, and meditate on the contents of this book. Even if you find yourself unable to agree with everything you encounter, I hope that you can nevertheless join me in the goal of mining from this unique Adventist proposition meaningful utility for the modern age.

To that end,

—— Pastor Marcos D. Torres

1.

Does the Pre-Advent Investigative Judgment Matter?

"Experience has shown, and a true philosophy will always show, that a vast, perhaps the larger, portion of truth arises from the seemingly irrelevant."
—— Edgar Allan Poe, *The Mystery of Marie Rogêt*

Every time Don Leatherman spoke, I found time stood still almost as if my consciousness was transplanted into an infinite realm. He lectured calmly, leaning back on an office chair while occasionally stroking his beard. There wasn't much charisma, but decades of scholarly wisdom undergirded just about everything he said, and I was hooked.

The year was 2014. I was a new theology student at Southern Adventist University and Dr. Don Leatherman was my Studies in Daniel lecturer.

Mesmerized, I frantically took as many notes as my mortal fingers allowed. I didn't miss a word save for the few times I got distracted by that guy watching basketball games on his laptop. Seriously, what was wrong with him? He was totally missing out.

The semester progressed and the class quickly made it to my "most awesome of all classes" list. We studied scholars, critics and the Glacier View document prepared by the late Dr. Desmond Ford. We also explored the structure of Daniel, its context and its objective. Dr. Leatherman even took the time to debunk some good old Adventist myths about the visions. Soon, we were required to select a topic for a research paper ranging from the historicity of Daniel and its authorship to its thematic structure and exegesis. But I didn't have a hard time choosing. My eyes were set on one topic and one topic only. As Dr. Leatherman went through the class asking for each student's choice, I silently begged that no one would steal mine. My wish came true and when, at last, he called my name. I answered: "The Pre-Advent Investigative Judgment" (henceforth PAIJ).

I chose the PAIJ because it was the one thing in Daniel, and in fact all of Adventism, that I wasn't convinced of. I wanted to know once and for all, is it Biblical? Or is it an Adventist fabrication designed to soften the blow of the Millerite disappointment? So, I got to work reading both critics and supporters. I wrestled with questions like, Is this doctrine taught in Daniel? Is it compatible with the gospel? Does it flow with the rest of scriptures narrative? Can it be demonstrated logically and rationally? And so forth. For me, the questions were of extreme value. Coupled with the heretical influence of Last Generation Theology, the doctrine of the PAIJ had caused me untold emotional and spiritual damage. I had little motivation to defend it or to find an excuse for its validity. I needed answers, and I was going to get them.

Nevertheless, there was a sense of trepidation. If I concluded that the doctrine was simply not defensible then, in the timeless words of the Hamlet character Polonius I would "to [mine] own self be true" meaning, at least in my estimation, that I might actually part ways with the church I had always called home. The thought was uncomfortable, but the lack of answers was worse. So, I picked my topic and got to work.

After tons of research and study, I submitted a 21-page paper in which I traced my journey toward not only concluding that the doctrine had biblical grounds but that I actually kind of really liked it. Dr. Leatherman replied that my paper exceeded the page limit but because he enjoyed it so much, he would not dock my grade. In addition, he added he would keep the paper in his file. I never actually told him, but for me that was the equivalent of a celebrity telling me they thought I was cool. I was on cloud nine.

Years have passed. Nothing has changed. I still place Studies in Daniel in my top 3 favorite classes of all time (right next to Biblical Exegesis and Adventist History). But the time has finally come for me to address the one thing about my experience with the PAIJ that I did not answer then nor for many years to follow. That question is simply this: *Why does any of it matter?*

Now you might be wondering, How could you write a 21 page paper and not address that foundational question? And my answer is I did. But the problem is, I also didn't. My excitement for the relevance of the PAIJ was built on the enthusiastic approach I had toward the entire course to begin with. As a result, the PAIJ was relevant to me because I was a bit of a theological nerd with a reasonable amount of theological baggage. But would it be relevant to anyone who didn't share my context? And to this day, as I navigate through life in a secular, Australian context I find that the relevance of a doctrine like the PAIJ is far from self-evident.

At this juncture, many would simply throw their hands up and say, "That's it! Doesn't matter! Let's just focus on the simple gospel and move on."

But not me and for two reasons. First, my mind doesn't work that way. I want to know, once and for all, does the PAIJ have anything meaningful to say to anyone who is not enamored with points of interpretation that have seemingly little to do with everyday life?

And second, the fact that the PAIJ appears to be irrelevant is not in itself a denunciation of the doctrine for that which is seemingly irrelevant can still emerge as fundamentally meaningful to the human experience. The laptop in my hands, for example, emerges as the conclusion to a series of processes I find utterly meaningless to contemplate. Likewise, I can type this paper on Google Docs thanks to a sequence of complex programing codes and engineering marvels that I would, likewise, think awfully tedious to ponder. Nothing about the laptop's assembly interests me and yet, the laptop itself is profoundly relevant in my life. In the same vein, when I look at a doctrine like the PAIJ, I cannot discount it simply because it appears irrelevant. I must, instead, explore the possibility that its irrelevant assembly may potentially effectuate something meaningful for the human experience; and what might that be? I certainly don't want to miss walking on the edge of something grand because I struggle to identify its immediate grandeur. I must then continue to explore for as the poet Edgar Allan Poe surmised, there are indeed times - more common than we think - when "truth arises from the seemingly irrelevant."

Therefore, in this article series "The Death and Rebirth of the Investigative Judgment" I want to submerge into the question, does the PAIJ matter? Is it relevant? Does it serve any other purpose besides the corporate identity we claim it provides us with? Or, to borrow from Andre Reis, does it simply "[massage] our corporate ego"?[1] This question of relevance will be the central focus of this entire article series.

But it is also necessary for me to explain what the series is not about. This series is not about whether the PAIJ is biblical. I am beginning from the assumption that it is and challenging its experiential utility from that starting point. Therefore, if you are convinced that the PAIJ is an unbiblical doctrine, this series offers no satisfaction to your contentions. This series is also not about whether the PAIJ contradicts the gospel. Plenty has been written to respond to those charges already and I have personally moved beyond that part of the conversation. Finally, this series is not about side issues related to the PAIJ such as Ellen White's relationship to the doctrine, exegetical questions concerning the meaning of certain texts or concepts in Leviticus or Hebrews. Those are issues that are, likewise, effectively dealt with elsewhere.

Therefore, the single focus of this series is, assuming the validity of the PAIJ what then is its utility?

There is a collective struggle with voices emerging each year that question this. These voices are often interpreted as mere critics, neo-Fordians who are unbending ideologues that can never be satisfied. But the truth is, at least from where I stand, we may actually be more at fault than we like to admit. Even I, a firm believer in this doctrine, must admit that we have struggled to provide truly compelling answers to begin with. Thus, at the end of our lengthy dissertations we can't seem to get away from the notion that, from the perspective of the non-academic, the PAIJ simply adds little to no significance to the overarching thematic evolution of scriptures narrative. To the academics, yes for the doctrine certainly resolves wrinkles and gaps left by the Arminian-Wesleyan tradition upon which Adventism is built. But is that enough to make it relevant for anyone else? It appears the answer is no.

There is also the individual struggle betrayed by the fact that most church members neither understand the doctrine nor care much for it. As a pastor, I have yet to find anyone who gets contagiously excited over it. It makes sense, yes. We can see the pieces click together, yes. But there is that annoying pragmatic challenge that keeps staring at us like an elephant in the room demanding an answer: What difference does it really make in my spiritual walk? If little to none, then what is the point of believing it? And perhaps this would not be a big deal if it was some obscure teaching that had little to do with our systematic, but the truth is, this doctrine is at the center of our identity! How terrible then that so few understand it or value it. Is the fault theirs? I think not. Rather, I am inclined to agree with Harold A. McGregor who wrote that the Investigative Judgement "remains an essentially indigestible aspect of Adventist teaching."[2]

Finally, there is the corporate struggle where the doctrine is held on to because it gives us some sense of identity and yet, if we are honest with ourselves, this uniquely held ideological construct has failed to produce in us anything exceptionally compelling or attractive in terms of actions or habits. Mahatma Gandhi captured the relationship between belief and habit well when he said, "Your beliefs become your thoughts, your thoughts become your words, your words become your actions, your actions become your habits..."[3]

In other words, a person's belief leads naturally to a change in a person's actions and habits. Ellen White expressed a nearly identical sentiment when she wrote, "If the thoughts are right, then as a result the words will be right; the actions will be of that character...."[4] Thus, if the PAIJ is deeply embedded in our belief as Adventists then one would expect to see something captivating in our actions and habits. Our unique doctrine would naturally lead us toward a unique expression of faith that is impossible to miss. And yet, we are not significantly more attractive than any other religious community. Our local churches are just as dead as most other ones. Our cultures are just as judgmental, cold, formal, traditional and stifled as other churches. We argue about the same things, get bogged down in the same nonsense and replicate the same brokenness as our contemporary societies. Racism, sexism and elitism, abuse, control and division are just as present among us as they are in people groups who do not hold anything remotely close to a doctrine like the PAIJ. And even when we get it right and show love, compassion and stand for justice in our communities we don't necessarily stand out. For a people who hold a belief no one else seems to hold, I find it odd that we perpetuate a culture everyone else seems to have. In other words, if the PAIJ matters in any way, shape or form then it is fair to expect its proponents to navigate reality in such a radically redemptive way that the whole world would take notice. But we don't.

Thus, George P. Saxon author of "The Investigative Judgment Really Ended in 1846" got it right when he asked,

> Does believing or not believing in the Investigative Judgment help or hinder you in your walk with Jesus? Should the investigative judgment be retained as a doctrine of the SDA Church? I would argue that this issue has been decided. Adventist ministers and administrators do not preach about this subject, and will not voluntarily discuss it. The younger Adventist population knows little or nothing about the Investigative Judgment. By their collective lack of interest the Adventist population has voted against it.[5]

So, where do we go from here? From a logical standpoint it appears we have only three options. The first is to maintain our course and allow the number of people who care about the PAIJ to continue to dwindle until only a small, nostalgic club remains. The second is to bow to the critics and either admit the whole thing was a sham or concede that despite its theological validity the doctrine has little to no experiential utility. And the third is to start over and find what, if anything, this fundamental notion has to offer to a fragmented culture wandering a path littered by the shards of daily suffering, naked and barefoot.

I suggest it's time we do the later and revisit this doctrine with a singular focus on its relevance. Can the question be adequately answered? I honestly don't know. The church has vacillated on this issue for so long, giving patriotic, immaterial and one dimensional answers to this multi-dimensional existentially driven question that we may very well be at a point in history in which the very mention of the PAIJ causes those who need this exploration the most to roll their eyes and walk the other way. And for good reason. They have already wasted enough time and gotten nowhere. Nevertheless, I believe providing a meaningful way forward will be of benefit to emerging generations, evangelistic efforts and the collective Adventist consciousness. And perhaps, the efficacy of each of these will bring meaning and value to the spaces we, as a global movement, inhabit.

But there is something more that drives this search, at least for me. And that something more is best captured by the words of late journalist Italo Calvino when he wrote, "A classic is a book that has never finished saying what it has to say."[6] Because the PAIJ has never, in my estimation, been adequately explored in terms of its relevance it sits there, as a man alone on his ethereal bench staring down at us. It stares at us, eyes wide open, begging to speak and say something of meaning and value to a moribund generation and yet it cannot speak. We must speak for it. We must be its voice. And yet, we have not. And in that sense, it appears to me as though the PAIJ is a doctrine that has not yet finished saying what it needs to say. We have robbed it of that pleasure by reducing its complexity to religio-centric arguments that satisfy our dogmatic agendas but we have yet to let it sing its song over the agony of the human experience, replete with its myriad of stories. And to this end, I am compelled to continue to explore because perhaps the problem with the PAIJ is not that it is, as the critics assert, a bankrupt ideology but that it is a classic that has not yet finished saying what it has to say.

Chapter Summary

- Despite having gained an impressive knowledge of the PAIJ's doctrinal anatomy, I continued to struggle with explaining why it mattered to others.

- Many supporters and critics of the PAIJ through the years have struggled with the same questions. Critics attack it as a doctrine that adds nothing to ones faith experience and is therefore false. Supporters have attempted to find meaning in the doctrine but many accept that despite what we have concocted, something is still missing.

- If we are going to discover meaning in the PAIJ it will require us to approach it from an entirely new perspective, asking entirely new questions of it, and allow it to speak its truth to us without the influence of tradition drowning out its voice.

Discussion Questions

1. Have you ever struggled with the meaning of the PAIJ? If so, how have you navigated that struggle?

2. What do you think of the statement "For a people who hold a belief no one else seems to hold (the PAIJ), I find it odd that we perpetuate a culture everyone else seems to have."

3. Why are you reading this book? What do you hope to find that you haven't found before?

Chapter Endnotes

1. Reis, Andre. "Perspective: 1844 -Pillar of Faith or Mortal Wound?" [Web: https://spectrummagazine.org/article/2015/10/22/perspective-1844-pillar-faith-or-mortal-wound]

2. McGregor Jr., Harold A. "The Investigative Judgment has Three Main Problems," [Web: https://spectrummagazine.org/article/harold-mcgregor-jr/2013/12/06/investigative-judgment-has-three-main-problems]

3. Brismar, Anna. "The Power of Thought," [Web: http://www.greenstrategy.se/the-power-of-thought-circular-fashion]

4. White, Ellen G. "Mind, Character and Personality," vol 2, p. 655

5. Saxon, George P. "The Investigative Judgment Really Ended in 1846," [Web: https://spectrummagazine.org/article/george-p-saxon/2012/09/12/investigative-judgment-really-ended-1846]

6. Calvino, Italo. As quoted in, "What Is Fiction For? Literary Humanism Restored," by Bernard Harrison p. 56.

2.

Why the Pre-Advent Investigative Judgment Doesn't Matter

"The saddest thing that could have happened to us, will be the saddest thing that could happen to us, and that is to become irrelevant."

—— S. H. Khan

Welcome back to part two of the series, "The Death and Rebirth of the Investigative Judgment". In the introduction, I asked the overarching question, "Does the Investigative Judgment Matter?" in which I demonstrated that even among those who support the doctrine, the question of its utility remains unsettled. In this second installment, I will demonstrate how the doctrine of the Investigative Judgment is, indeed, dead and how our greatest defenses of the subject repeatedly come short. In doing so, I aim to lay the necessary foundation for its rebirth.

In his book, "Recovery: Freedom from Our Addictions" comedian Russell Brand asks the thought-provoking question, "What is a belief really?" And his answer is awfully uncomfortable. A belief, he says, is "a thought in your mind that you like having." He then makes matters worse by adding, "If you like having it, it must be of benefit, it either improves your life or helps you to rationalize how bad your life is."[1]

From an epistemic perspective, I find his definition facile. But from a practical, day to day point of view, it's spot on. People tend to believe what they believe because the belief adds something of value. When a belief does not add value, we either ignore it, minimize it or get rid of it. Therefore, when discussing the utility of a belief like the Pre-Advent Investigative Judgment (PAIJ) I am forced to ask, *Why* do I believe this?

However, the answers to this question are surprisingly complex. On the one hand, the PAIJ benefits me academically. Once I understood its mechanics, I found it provided me with a coherent systematic theology unlike anything I had encountered before. Because I was aware of the intricacies and discontinuities present in the Arminian and Calvinist theological debates, Adventism, with its sanctuary, PAIJ and 1844 doctrines, ironed out wrinkles and brought the narrative of scripture together in a way those other systems could not.[2] However, despite its academic usefulness, I cannot say it has ever held any defining status in my personal life.[3]

Consequently, the question that has haunted me for years is - what if I wasn't into theology? What if I was just a simple guy wandering through the balefulness of existence hoping to scoop up a few crumbs of meaning from whatever sensory experience I found next? Or what if I was just a simple Christian navigating the maze of life via the promise and power of the gospel? No theology. No background in dizzying church debates. No knowledge of how Plato and Aristotle impacted the development of classical Christian thought. No investment in the war between free will and sovereignty and zero concern for denominational propaganda. And what if, as either of these persons, I was approached by an Adventist and asked to join their church? Perhaps I would lean towards a "yes" because of Adventist doctrines like annihilationism, Sabbath or the holistic view of man, but what significant role would the PAIJ play? For a doctrine that is supposed to be intricately woven into our identity, I struggle to see how it would tip the scales for me in terms of choosing to join the Adventist church.

But that's not to say I haven't tried answering the question. In fact, I have historically offered three key perspectives when it comes to the question of the PAIJ's relevance. These three key perspectives are not original to me but represent, after mountains of research, the absolute best I could gather from the scholars and theologians.

The Transparency Argument

The first is that the PAIJ makes no sense outside of an Arminian-Wesleyan metanarrative. This system of thought is the foundation for Adventism's "Great Controversy". When we consider, as clinical psychologist Jordan Peterson often affirms, that "life is suffering", or to quote the first noble truth of Buddhism, "existence is suffering", then the Great Controversy theme emerges as a compelling solution to the apparent contradiction between God's love and our present, wretched experience. Such is life in a reality deconstructed by the presence of the absence of God. There is hope, yes. But the hope must be held before us, a light at the end of the tunnel to guide us, for the truth is we are still in the tunnel and it is cold and dark and the ground beneath soaked in the blood and tears of God and men. This is the Great Controversy.

And as the Great Controversy draws to a close, God must author the epilogue, preceded by judgment. For his people, this judgment is bathed in enthusiastic and romantic expectation. For his enemies, it is a portend of inexorable ruin. But how does this God of love conduct his judgment? The PAIJ reveals that he does so with transparency. And this transparency is, in and of itself, incalculably meaningful.

Does such an idea provide relevance to the doctrine of the PAIJ? To a certain degree, yes. Only an ideologue with a chip on his shoulder, unable to suspend his own preconceived antithesis, would deny this. But while this may be the case in a theological sense, the truth is very few people stay awake at night wondering if God is transparent. Most people are content to accept his love and leave the rest in his hands. Various theological systems may deny this love and transparency of God, but few people are navigating theology at the depth necessary to make understanding a theme like divine transparency vital. So, while the PAIJ finds a certain degree of relevance in the way in which it celebrates the transparency of God, the very theme of God's transparency is not one a person is likely to explore unless they are a theological pundit of some sort.

Benefit for the Angels

The second perspective I have historically offered is that, given the Great Controversy, the PAIJ becomes indispensable to the angelic realm. It is not simply us that God is transparent with but all of his sentient creation. In the PAIJ, the angels are able to see for themselves that God's judgments are just and true. This idea is then tied into the overarching theme of the Great Controversy and the uncertainties the struggle between good and evil is rooted in. A traditional perspective proposes that the angels, emotionally and cognitively impacted by the initial rebellion and its aftermath, would be within their rights to demand an assurance that this rebellion will not happen again. This involves God celebrating the character of his redeemed whom he is bringing into eternity. By putting them on display before the angels through the process of the PAIJ, he assures them that all who are entering his kingdom are authentic beings who, through imperfect and damaged by sin, have no allegiance to its regime and are, indeed, reborn into the new humanity of which Christ is head.

This conceptualisation of the PAIJ also gives the doctrine a level of relevance. It paints a picture of God's government as driven by open discussion instead of coercive power. The angels are postulated in a deliberative and potentially representative symposium. We can confidently assert a level of debate, inquisitive dialogue and autonomous exploration. There is no room for anecdotes or conjecture. God's own judgment is dissected, not with incredulous skepticism but with a sacred consciousness and awe. Some find this idea appalling given the loving nature of God. Why would the angels be engaged in such a process? Don't they trust the love of the Father? The answer to this question is simple and complex. Complex because we don't understand the layers upon which angelic society functions. Simple because, despite this ignorance we need only look at ourselves to know that love, while foundationally sufficient, must be expressed in tangible ways that transcend romantic platitudes. To this end, I find the words of the anti-totalitarian novelist George Orwell insightful when he wrote, "Perhaps one did not want to be loved so much as to be understood."[4]

Though the setting in which these words were written differ from our present topic, nevertheless they capture something beautiful that can be appropriated for this moment. In keeping with Orwell's contrast between the act of being loved and being understood, we can see how the PAIJ leaps forth with meaning, particularly against the backdrop of the 20th century's political legacy, marred by the likes of Stalin, Hitler and Mao Zedong. By way of variance, the PAIJ reveals that God doesn't simply love his intelligent creation but nurtures an anti-totalitarian process in which they can feel heard, their sufferings acknowledged, and their concerns intentionally understood. Revelation 20:4 depicts the Great White throne judgment the same way - as transparent and meaningful for the created order and not just a process that takes place within God's enigmatic and inscrutable consciousness.

However, as we will explore in more detail in the next article, the problem is if this perspective is true then at best it demonstrates why the PAIJ is relevant for heavenly beings. It does less to demonstrate why it is relevant for us. A person would first have to wonder about the angelic perspective on judgment before this perspective has any value, and sadly, no one outside of theological circles ever does. Thus, in a sense, this position answers a question no one is really asking.

Vindication of God's Character

Finally, the third answer I have offered is in reference to the character of God. Because the Great Controversy understands the war between good and evil as a war that is fundamentally rooted in lies about God then the judgment, we understand, is part of what exonerates God's character before the universe. Those from a reformed/ Calvinist background would find this idea disturbing. In this system of thought, God does whatever he pleases without any need to explain himself. However, outside of this system of thought the idea of God vindicating his character has potentiality for spiritual and emotional healing as has been documented by Adventist psychiatrist Timothy Jennings and physician Neil Nedley. Likewise, the idea of God vindicating himself was brought into the micro-level of human experience in William P. Young's classic novel "The Shack". Despite its theological challenges, one particularly insightful and touching scene in the story is when the main character sits in judgment over God only to discover the goodness of God as a result.

The PAIJ is part of this vindication narrative. And like the above novel's protagonist, humanity lives in a perpetual state of judgment over God. We question his motives, dissect his decisions and, as was cleverly expressed in the 2003 film "Bruce Almighty", we think ourselves capable of doing a much better job. Therefore, the idea of God being vindicated before the universe is one that has theological and, as already expressed, psychological benefits. Following on from this, the relevance of the PAIJ as it relates to the vindication of God's character becomes extraordinarily significant.

However, the doctrine once again runs into problems that, while not denying its validity add to its struggle for utility. The first is that it's just too complicated a doctrine. A person first has to swim through miles of charts, dates and ancient cultic metaphors before they can arrive at the vindication narrative. As a result, while the doctrine certainly amplifies the goodness of God's character, it does so at such a complex level that the amplification gets lost in translation. The end result I have seen is pastors who emphasise the overarching themes of God's character and goodness but avoid the PAIJ in the process. The second is that the goodness of God's character is mere ideological noise if not accompanied by practical, on the ground application. Sadly, the greatest argument against the PAIJ is its apparent silence in terms of meaningful, social effect both within our church and in the communities our movement inhabits.

Other less convincing arguments I have toyed with are how the PAIJ gives Adventism a purpose and identity (this argument fails to provide any meaning to anyone who is not already an Adventist), how it protects us from both legalism and antinomianism at the same time (a person has to first care about that tension to find meaning in the doctrine), how the prophetic timeline ending in 1844 intensifies our belief in the soon coming of Jesus (while true, this idea serves only as a temporary boost to the emotion that has little lasting effect on a person's faith), and how it reveals to us what Jesus has been up to throughout human history to this very moment (knowing all the ins-and-outs of the High Priestly ministry does not lead us, on a practical level, to a faith experience that is any different from that of other Christians who do not share this belief).

So, do I believe in the PAIJ or do I not? The answer is simple: I believe in its validity but struggle with its utility. To this day, I have found all of our traditional arguments in favor of the PAIJ to be desperately impoverished in the realm of everyday efficacy. It's not that the arguments are inherently bad. In fact, they each teeter on the edge of cosmic and local significance. The problem is that, despite the value they bring to the conversation, it's simply not enough. Something is still missing that we have yet to identify and explore. As a result, after years of studying the Bible with a wide diversity of students, I have never been asked a question of any kind that is conclusively or compellingly answered by the PAIJ as we know it today. To the contrary, I have taught the doctrine with an impressive knowledge of its anatomy. And yet, I have suffered at its seemingly pointless existence. In a sense, Adventism's conceptualisation of the PAIJ has become the fulfilment of Lewis Carroll's novel "Through the Looking Glass" in which the heroine Alice finds herself running as fast as she can only to be told by the Red Queen, "Now, here, you see, it takes all the running you can do, to keep in the same place."[5]

I believe this "Red Queen Effect" has kept us sprinting in a theological marathon for over 170 years, but we have gone nowhere. As a result, we have collectively entered the sad state of affairs S. H. Khan refers to as "to become irrelevant." Books, sermons and articles defending the PAIJ as a cornerstone of Adventism simply fail, over and over again, to say anything truly meaningful to anyone who is not already an "us". Similarly, the complexity of the doctrine continues to elude any practical, world constructing influence that cannot be found in communities of faith bereft of the PAIJ. Our church members also continue to struggle with the doctrines meaning and, apart from a few studious bookworms, most can hardly explain it. It is this present reality that leads me to conclude that the PAIJ is a doctrine that is, despite all our efforts, dead. And what does the future then hold for us and our collective mission? Though I refrain from speculation I can affirm, in the heedful words of Chinese philosopher and poet Lao Tzu, that "If [we] do not change direction [we] may end up where [we] are heading."[6]

Nevertheless, I contend that a rebirth lies before us for I have found that the death of the PAIJ is not rooted in a terminal flaw in the doctrine itself, but rather in the way which we, its proponents, have framed it and defended it. Our efforts, proud as we may be of them, have fallen short and left entire generations with little to no connection with the one doctrine we claim as our contribution to the global conversation about God. And yet, beneath the dust of futile argumentation lies a potentiality yet to be realized and set free.

So then, what is the way forward? Where do we go from here? If our traditional arguments defending the relevance of the PAIJ have fallen short, then what options do we have left?

Danish philosopher Soren Kierkegaard once said, "Life can only be understood backwards; but it must be lived forwards."[7] His point is that in order for life to have meaning it must exist in tension with what is behind and what lies ahead. By looking backwards, we can make sense of the complexity of self, learn from our mistakes and construct perspective. By looking forward we can journey with enthusiasm and be driven by the existential dream of redemption. This tension is therefore necessary to thrive into one's authentic self and, ironically, to live a life that is greater than that self. And it is this tension that I believe is necessary for Adventism if it wishes to speak life into the culture. We must pursue a more relevant understanding and conceptualisation of the PAIJ, informed by the narrative behind and driven by a vision of the future that transcends our own corporate identity. This approach, I believe, will allow us to finally extract the hidden potential embedded in this landmark doctrine. A potential which has the capacity to speak life over the brokenness of the human story and offer a perspective that is relevant, cross-centered and captivating in its amplification of God's relentless love.

Chapter Summary

- Traditional Adventist answers regarding the PAIJ's meaning are sound and valid. However, they fail to address concerns everyday people have. As a result the doctrine ends up being of interest and use only to those who are already immersed in theological tensions not relevant to the general public.

- Failure to think outside the box and construct an approach to the PAIJ that transcends its historic framework is at the foundation of the PAIJ's pragmatic death.

- In order for the PAIJ to be reborn, we must allow our exploration to be informed by the past while pushing on toward new, unexplored possibilities.

Group Discussion

1. How do you feel about the traditional, historic framework for the PAIJ?

2. Do you agree with the proposition that the traditional framework is true and beautiful, but that it must be built on in order for the doctrine to continue to speak beyond its historic voice?

3. How confident are you that the doctrine of the PAIJ – properly reframed – can ignite passion and purpose in our local churches?

Chapter Endnotes

1. Brand, Russel. "Recovery: Freedom from our Addictions," p. 68

2. To explore how the PAIJ resolves the tensions present in the Arminian/ Calvinist theological debates see 1. Manea, Mike. "Why the Critics of the Investigative Judgment Have Failed," [Web: https://thecompassmagazine.com/blog/why-the-critics-of-the-investigative-judgment-have-failed] and 2. Manea, Mike. "How Adventism Ended the Gospel Wars," [Web: https://thecompassmagazine.com/blog/how-adventism-ended-the-gospel-wars]

3. In fact, the only time it did hold overwhelming significance is when the doctrine was tied to perfectionism and I lived each day in fear that I had to attain absolute character perfection or be lost forever. For all the faults in this heretical line of thinking, I must admit, it gives the 1844 IJ an intensity and value that can't be ignored. The doctrine becomes an integral part of how life is lived each day. Grant it, you might end up with an anxiety disorder, but at least you don't have to wonder what role the doctrine is meant to play.

4. Orwell, George. "1984," [web: http://www.george-orwell.org/1984/18.html]

5. Farnam Street, "The Red Queen Effect: Avoid Running Faster and Faster Only to Stay in the Same

Place," [web: https://fs.blog/2012/10/the-red-queen-effect]

6. Lao Tzu, as quoted in: Johnson, Patrick. ""If you do not change direction, you may end up...", [Web: http://beyondquarterlife.com/change-direction-may-end]

7. "Søren Kierkegaard," [Web: https://en.wikiquote.org/wiki/S%C3%B8ren_Kierkegaard]

3.

What Makes a Thing matter?

"Relevance changes over time."
———— Wes Trochill

In the first article of this series we explored the decaying contemporary milieu of the Pre-Advent Investigative Judgment (PAIJ). In the second installment we dove into Adventism's collective failure to extrapolate world-changing potential from the doctrine resulting in its practical, on-the-ground demise. Consequently, the doctrine lacks relevance to anyone who is not an "us" and even then, its usefulness appears to be reserved for the tiny substrate of church members who enjoy theological investigation. Thus, as far as the average population of the church is concerned, the PAIJ holds little to no meaning. Its utility is placed under greater scrutiny in a non-Adventist context (such as secular, post-Christian society) which is neither challenged nor inspired by the doctrines proposed ideological and theological contributions.

But is this quandary inherent to the doctrine itself? Or is the blame on us? In this third segment of "The Death and Rebirth of the Investigative Judgment" I will argue that the fault lies squarely in our conceptualisation of the PAIJ and not in its essence. In fact, as I will later demonstrate, the essence of the doctrine has been altogether missed in favor of outdated and surface argumentation that, while offering glimpses of meaning and value, simply teeter on the edge of its actualization without ever truly diving in.

Before we arrive at that conclusion though, we need to step out of the theological world and explore a more fundamental question: What exactly is relevance? The answer is imperative to laying the necessary foundation for the rebirth of the PAIJ. In fact, I find it odd that in all our attempts to make the doctrine relevant we have never once defined exactly what it is we mean by relevance. The assumption has been that a relevant thing is a thing that matters. And so, we embark on a crusade for any and every possible excuse we can find to say, "See? This is why the PAIJ matters!" But relevance goes a lot deeper than merely finding justifications for something to exist. Therefore, before continuing the theological conversation over the PAIJ, let us turn our attention to the very concept of relevance itself.

What is Relevance?

According to the Cambridge Dictionary, relevance is "the degree to which something is related or useful to what is happening or being talked about".[1] At first glance, this definition does not appear to offer anything different from our instinctive perception of what relevance is. If a thing is interesting to a certain group of people, then it is relevant to them. And if it is not interesting, we must find ways of making it so. This, I observe, has been our historic approach. However, if we return to Cambridge's definition, we find a formula composed of two simple foundations. The first is that there is a thing being talked about and the second, that there is a thing that relates to the thing being talked about. The interaction of these two elements gives birth to relevance.

In other words, relevance is not a concept that exists in isolation. Instead, relevance is always derivative. Likewise, relevance does not lead a conversation but follows it. It does not introduce ideas but, to the contrary, adds or subtracts from them. Therefore, a potential way of formulating the nature of relevance is to conceptualize two layers of ideas. The first we can refer to as the "primary idea" and the second simply the "secondary idea". It would look something like this:

Primary Idea + Secondary Idea = Relevance

As can be seen above, relevance emerges in relation to an existing primary idea. This means that no secondary idea is ever relevant or meaningful unless it relates to an already existing primary idea (the nature of how primary ideas come to be is beyond the scope of this series). Thus, any idea introduced that does not relate to a primary idea is irrelevant while the ideas that do relate by adding or subtracting from the primary idea, are the ones that are considered relevant.[2]

For example, imagine you are discussing your favorite food with a friend and it happens to be pizza. Your friend then responds by saying they have a friend who lives in Chicago. The secondary idea introduced by your friend is really no secondary idea at all. That is, it has nothing to do with the primary idea of liking pizza. It adds nothing to that idea and neither does it subtract from it. Therefore, your friend introducing a new idea about a friend living in Chicago is irrelevant to the primary idea that is already in motion and, as a result, is meaningless.

However, if your friend said, "I have a friend who lives in Chicago and he owns his own pizza restaurant," now we have a secondary idea. It ties into the primary idea already in motion and adds to it. In your primary idea you are saying that pizza is the best food. Your friend then introduces a secondary idea in the form of an anecdote which adds content and value to your primary idea. Consequently, the secondary idea is relevant and, as more relevant secondary ideas are introduced, the conversation thrives.

But why is this important to understand? The answer is simple. Relevance is not found in simply introducing justification for an idea. Psychology lecturer Robin Robertson expressed this best when she wrote, "Many attempt to add relevance to otherwise uninteresting content by focusing efforts on creating interest." She then goes on to identify the different ways people attempt to do this and concludes that unless a person finds the content "worth knowing, then their attention will likely wane."[3] And in order for an idea to be "worth knowing" the idea itself must necessarily relate to a primary idea already in motion. If it does not, you can justify the existence of your idea all you want but, in the end, none of what you say will add any value to the conversations already taking place. Therefore, after much effort your idea will still prove to be irrelevant for it does not, in its very essence, add meaning to any primary ideas that are already occupying societies attention.

How this Applies to the PAIJ

Now that we understand the nature of relevance let us return to the theological discussion about the PAIJ. The reason why the PAIJ lacks relevance is that, for all the work we have done to justify its existence, nothing that the doctrine represents adds any value to societies existing primary ideas. As I said in article two, the doctrine appears to have the most meaning to those in academic and theological circles. This is due to the fact that theologians, particularly Adventist ones, already have a vested interest in the doctrine. Consequently, defending the PAIJ is a primary idea already in motion in our lives. Thus, when we find secondary ideas that bolster this *a priori* commitment we attribute value to those secondary ideas that those outside of our field would not. We then introduce those secondary ideas to the church, composed of people who are not engaged in the primary idea of the PAIJ's utility, and our brilliant ideas fall flat. Even when positively embraced, we cannot help but admit that they are not consequential to our spiritual experience as we would like them to be.

Therefore, if we want the PAIJ to be relevant to the church and, ultimately, to the culture then we must revisit the doctrine from an entirely different perspective - one that speaks life into the already ongoing primary ideas in the world and in the culture. To continue to defend the PAIJ based on secondary ideas that speak life to primary ideas only theologians care about is the very reason we are in the conundrum we find ourselves in. We must celebrate the foundation we have built so far but likewise admit the journey is not over. At best, everything we have discovered about the PAIJ has simply served to lay a foundation of raw materials. We have yet to construct something meaningful on that foundation. And I propose we never will until we begin to look at the doctrine as a secondary idea that is intended to add to or subtract from primary ideas found not only in our theological ivory towers, but in the collective human experience.

This pattern of Biblical secondary ideas adding or subtracting to social primary ideas is not new. In fact, it is how theology functions on a pragmatic level. The cross is relevant across time and culture because it speaks to the shared perspective of the redemption of being - a primary idea felt everywhere. The state of the dead is relevant because it too speaks to the primary idea of death, afterlife and the nature of being. That is, these are conversations already taking place that the doctrine then adds and subtracts variables from. We also have the doctrine of God, the doctrine of the church, the doctrine of last things and the doctrine of heaven all of which speak secondary ideas into already existing questions over origins, destiny, family and society. But turn your attention now to the PAIJ and ask, what primary ideas does it address? If you are a staunch supporter of the doctrine, perhaps you will fish something out of thin air. But if you are willing to admit the struggle, you will find that the PAIJ speaks little into existing societal concerns.

Why is the PAIJ Disconnected from Society's Primary Ideas?

So why is the PAIJ irrelevant in the realm of contemporary primary ideas? The answer is simple - it does not add or subtract from any contemporary concerns. This is the consequence of force fitting the doctrine into a religious and corporate packaging that gives us as sense of grandiose fulfillment but, by default, offers nothing to the world beyond the "us".

On the religious constraints, it is easy to see that the PAIJ is a doctrine constructed on two simple foundations - Arminian theology and soul sleep. Unlike Calvinism, Arminianism embraces human free will and presents the probability of a person being lost after salvation (Arminian theology rejects the concepts of "Once Saved Always Saved" and the Calvinist doctrine of predestination). Because of this, all Arminians believe that believers are judged after death as their soul is transported to heaven. However, because Adventists don't believe in the immortal soul, we believe that a person is unconscious in death which means the judgment takes place, not at death, but at a particular point in history. Without continuing down that rabbit hole, suffice to say that in this setting the PAIJ has religious value because it explains how God differentiates between the saved and the lost - including those who professed Christ and later rejected him. Thus, this entire framework of the PAIJ basically revolves around whether a person was faithful to the end or not and provides answers to religious questions about assurance, perseverance and judgment that other Arminian denominations (Pentecostals, Methodists, Arminian Baptists etc.) have never been able to formulate.

However important this framework may be for theological and systematic discussion; it is a meaningless framework for the average Christian and even less relevant for the culture. In addition, the preoccupation with these things does not lead to a practical Christian life not already available to someone who is pursuing an authentic spiritual walk with God. Thus, this framework, while valuable in academia, is increasingly meaningless in evangelism, discipleship and mission especially in our post to meta-modern transitional age.[4]

In order to move forward then, we must transcend our traditional frameworks which naturally invites us to lay aside our own desire for religious and institutional affirmation. The doctrine of the PAIJ does not exist to give us a corporate identity that we use to pacify our sense of importance. Likewise, it does not exist to iron out theological wrinkles that scholars have been splitting hairs over for centuries. Rather, it exists to communicate something of value about God's heart into the human experience.

When we think back to our pioneers, we can see that a primary idea in motion for them was the great disappointment of October 22, 1844. This disappointment occupied emotional and existential energy that, for some, demanded a resolution. When the doctrine of the PAIJ came to light, it emerged as a secondary idea that brought resolution to an already existing primary idea - the disappointment.

As valid as this position may be, we must admit that the disappointment is no longer an active primary idea. No one is investing emotional and existential energy into resolving the puzzle of a failed prediction in 1844. We simply live too far removed from the events to have any intimate connection to them. Thus, by virtue of the passage of time the primary idea of the disappointment is no longer important. As consultant Wes Trochill so aptly pointed out, "relevance changes over time."[5]

Nevertheless, Adventists continue to defend the relevance of the PAIJ on the basis that it answers the question of the disappointment. I do not disagree with the argument in a historical or theological sense. It is certainly valid. But such a line of reason provides zero utility to the doctrine today because the disappointment is simply not a primary idea anymore. Thus, when we base the relevance of the PAIJ on the secondary idea of "making sense of the disappointment" we base its relevance on an idea that has zero value in contemporary society.

Likewise, the early Adventists were immersed in the war between Arminian and Calvinist theology. This battle tended to revolve around matters such as free-will, assurance of salvation, the place of the law, the nature of death and the human soul, the role of obedience, sanctification and covenant theology. In addition, new theological concepts began to emerge, such as Dispensational theology, which argued vehemently against any positive posture toward the law of God (a posture all classical protestants share, not just Adventists[6]). These developments were alarming because, for the first time, the fringe antinomian sentiment of generations past appeared to be systematizing itself into a theology that competed with the classical systems of Protestant thought. Add to these tensions the fact that most of Adventism's audience in North America was already Christian and you have the building blocks for a very relevant conceptualisation of the PAIJ that answered questions related to each of these religious debates occupying the primary ideas of many.

Fast forward to the aftermath of World War 1 and the emergence of post-modernism and suddenly, the primary ideas our pioneers were interacting with no longer exist. Society grows increasingly secular. Theological evangelical debates are progressively sidelined. A cynical and skeptical view of the future, of the nature of reality and of the very concept of truth begin to dominate the cultural consciousness. The death of God prognosticated by the German philosopher Friedrich Nietzsche and popularized in his novel "Thus Spoke Zarathustra" gained increasing credibility. Thus, by 1961 the French theologian Gabriel Vahanian could argue for the secularization of Western society in his classic, "The Death of God: The Culture of Our Post-Christian Era" in which he stated,

> [M]odern culture is gradually losing the marks of that Christianity which brought it into being and shaped it. Whether from a national or an international perspective, Christianity has long

since ceased to be coextensive with our culture...[7]

Vahanian's observation was, of course, preceded by momentous episodes in the story of humanity. The Great Depression, World War 2 and the Cold War, accompanied by the "Red Scare" had left an indelible mark on society that reshaped the existential priorities of the culture. Thus, Vahanian was right in observing that the primary ideas of the day had moved far from the biblical and into the socio-political. Less and less people cared about Arminian and Calvinist debates anymore. The endless banter between law and grace seemed laughable. The culture moved increasingly toward the post-Christianity described by Vahanian. The world was moving at a hundred miles an hour with society changing at an unprecedented pace. Today, that transition is in full effect on the heels of incredible technological advancement on the one hand, and a subconscious trauma implanted onto us by acts of terrorism, mass murder and international war. In the midst of this, emerging generations increasingly identify as religious "none's" - spiritual yes, but far removed from any semblance of historic Christian faith.[8]

And Adventism rides along in the background. The doctrine of the PAIJ seemingly untouched. It maintains its old framework fueled by the primary ideas of a bygone century. It said nothing to the struggle for equality. It remained silent in the face of Jim Crow. In fact, the very people who hold to this unique doctrinal construct turn out to be no different to the culture, perpetuating the racial inequality of fallen man within our own denomination.[9] The PAIJ rides on. It utters no encouragement or enlightenment to the Civil Rights movement. It offers no resistance to the totalitarian, communist threat. It gives humanity no hope in the light of Hiroshima and the peril of complete self-annihilation. It simply keeps its old framework and to this day, the PAIJ remains locked in the ideological constructs of our pioneers. The constructs were good yes, and they still remain true and valid. But has the PAIJ nothing more to say? Did its capacity to speak to contemporary primary ideas die with our pioneers? Or is it, as I imagined, as a lone man sitting on an ethereal bench staring at us, his heart beating, longing to say something of meaning to the human experience, and yet he is silenced by our own incredulity and inability to think higher, further and wider than the basic raw materials gifted to us by our forefathers?

Failure to do any of the above has resulted in a doctrine that tends to be more of an ancient ideological artifact than a present, world changing concept. It also explains why our best arguments have fallen short. As valid as the transparency of God is as a theological concept, it simply adds little to existing primary ideas. Likewise, the benefit for the angel's motif is essentially a secondary idea that relates to primary ideas in heaven, not on earth. Finally, while the vindication of God holds the most meaning of all the arguments, it has not been framed in a compelling way that addresses the cries of the cultures heart.

The doctrine is dead, ladies and gentlemen, but it can be reborn. There is but one prerequisite. We must be willing to be led by it and to overcome the compulsion of control that we have oppressed it with for so long. We must let the doctrine speak and then, we must take its message and speak on its behalf. It is not a deconstruction that we need, for in the words of WF Buckley, the ancient ideas are not anachronistic. Rather, the "the idiom of life is always changing" and we must be prepared to adapt. And when we do, we will then be poised to offer a relevant message to an erratic and broken generation finding comfort in the digital Asherah poles of the day, longing for connection and meaning in a world of convenience and consumerism, mindless violence and mass, unjustifiable death, all while crying out against the cynical irony of its forerunners with a longing for something, anything better.

In the next article, I will introduce a potential reframing of the PAIJ that is not only rooted in the text but that also speaks meaning into universal primary ideas. These universals are primary ideas that humanity has already actuated and is attempting to resolve everywhere. I will also show examples of how the PAIJ could have been of incalculable meaning in generations past and yet, missed its opportunity because of the frameworks it was locked into. This will serve as a warning for the future of our denomination and also as an encouragement built, not on self-idealizing propaganda but on a narrative that lifts Jesus up before a desperate and vagabond civilization.

Chapter Summary

- Relevance never leads a discussion but follows it. A thing is relevant only when it relates and adds value to an already existing idea.

- The reason why the PAIJ has lost relevance is because its historic framework added value to the historic ideas that surrounded it. Today, its historic framework interacts with ideas that no longer occupy the cultural consciousness.

- In order for the PAIJ to have relevance in the modern age, we must build on its historic framework toward a contemporary one that relates to and adds value to contemporary ideas.

Discussion Questions

1. How does the nature of relevance interact with our need, as a church, to adapt and update our message to speak meaningfully to emerging generations?

2. Can you identify any other doctrines that suffer the same "relevance issues" in our church? Which are they and how can we reframe them to speak meaningfully to contemporary primary ideas?

3. Get creative and share some ways in which you personally think the PAIJ can be reframed from its historic framework toward a contemporary one that interacts with the conversations that currently dominate our culture.

Chapter Endnotes

1. Cambridge Dictionary, Online. [Web: https://dictionary.cambridge.org/dictionary/english/relevance]

2. This particular definition of relevance is what I refer to as "pragmatic relevance" in that it accepts the existence of primary ideas and searches for practical ways to connect secondary ideas to those already existing primaries. A typical approach among conservative Christians though is to argue that a thing is relevant by virtue of its inherent value regardless of how it connects to a primary idea or not. This approach leads to a definition of relevance I refer to as "dogmatic relevance" in which no attempt at Contextualisation is made because the proponent of the idea thinks it unnecessary to reframe. In this model primary ideas are ignored on the basis that people should believe the secondary idea by virtue of its inherent value. This approach, however, ignores practical concerns and takes one a more coercive tone that ultimately fails to accomplish its intended aim.

3. Roberson, Robin. "Helping Students Find Relevance," [Web: https://www.apa.org/ed/precollege/ptn/2013/09/students-relevance]

4. This does not mean that the framework is useless or faulty. In fact, I personally engage in these very

frameworks with theologians and have a high level of interest in resolving them. What it simply means then is that once this framework is ironed out in academic theology, it must then be reframed into a meaningful message for the general public. In short, the issues debated and resolved in academia are not always meaningful to people at face value.

5. Trochill, Wes. "Relevance is the Key to Understanding Your Audience," [Web: https://effectivedatabase.com/relevance-is-the-key-to-understanding-your-audience]

6. See: Torres, Marcos D. "The Hole in Adventism: Making Total Sense of the Old & New Covenant," at https://www.thestorychurchproject.com/store1

7. Vahanian, Gabriel. "The Death of God: The Culture Of Our Post Christian Era," p. 228 [Web: https://archive.org/stream/deathofgodthecul012946 mbp/deathofgodthecul012946mbp_djvu.txt]

8. For more see, "The Rise of the Nones: Understanding and Reaching the Religiously Unaffiliated," by James Emery White.

9. See: "Against the Wall" at https://againstthewall.org

4.

Reframing the Pre-Advent Investigative Judgment

"The snake which cannot cast its skin has to die. As well the minds which are prevented from changing their opinions; they cease to be mind."

—— Friedrich Nietzsche

Welcome to the most anticipated article in "The Death and Rebirth of the Investigative Judgment" series. Up to this point, we have merely explored the empirical death of the landmark Adventist doctrine known as the Pre-Advent Investigative Judgment (PAIJ). That death, I have argued, is not due to a mortal flaw in the doctrine itself but in our collective failure to allow the doctrine to transcend its historic framework. This failure is due to many factors that I have not attempted to explore, but suffice to say, Adventism has constricted the PAIJ into a religious box that interacts with religious concerns and makes sense only within a religious cosmology that is regarded as meaningful only by those who self-identify as already belonging to a religious (a specifically Adventist one) community. This narrow ideological fabric has resulted in the catastrophic demise of the one doctrine we hold as our most unique contribution to theology. However, if released from this constriction, I contend that we will discover the foundation for its rebirth. That rebirth is what this present article is all about.

Before I begin, I want to make two things clear. First, I am not a deconstructionist. Unlike many critics of the PAIJ whom assert the doctrine has been wrong all along, I happen to believe we have been right. At no point do I question the validity of our historic understanding of the PAIJ.[1] So in this present article, I am not calling for a deconstruction of the doctrine in which we throw away all we have built in favor of some new, unheard of formulation. To the contrary, as I mentioned in article two (based on Kierkegaard's view of past and future in tension) we must look to our historic understanding in order to build the future. Therefore, at no point do I advocate or even claim camaraderie with anyone who seeks to abandon our historic position.

Second, because I am building on our historic foundation, the present article simply explores how to contextualise, or reframe, the PAIJ in a way that speaks to universal primary ideas. Perhaps the best way to understand this is to picture our understanding of the PAIJ in three layers. The first layer introduces the doctrine in connection with universal primary ideas (more on this to come), with simplicity and with applicatory power. The second layer digs even deeper by exploring the rich symbolism, typology and archetypes associated with the PAIJ. It explores the sanctuary in depth (its cultic rituals, architecture, art) along with its metaphysical origins and meaning as well as its soteriological and eschatological implications. This third layer is the final layer of intricacy and amplifies the doctrines utility even more by exploring its contribution to Christian theology and how it resolves important issues in the debate over Christian theology. In doing so, it expands on the PAIJ's meaning and relevance (these will be briefly explored in the next article).

The problem with Adventism that I am aiming to resolve is we tend to introduce people to the PAIJ at the third layer. Those who are lucky eventually find the second layer. But very few, if any, ever encounter the doctrine at the first layer. I propose we do it backwards (which is really the right way) and introduce people to the doctrine at the first layer. This means it must connect to a universal primary idea, be simple enough for even a child to comprehend, and have applicatory power. This first layer is the one we must use in evangelism, Bible studies etc. The second and third layer are reserved for deeper study as the convert continues to explore in the years that follow baptism.

With those preliminary considerations out of the way, I want to turn our attention over to the reframing of the PAIJ with the simple question, Is reframing itself even biblical?

Is Reframing a Doctrine Biblical?

The primary fear associated with "reframing doctrine" is that by virtue of the act itself, we may end up destroying the thing we think we are saving. Consequently, many approach the attempt itself with suspicion. Therefore, before fully diving in I would like to calm those fears by turning over to scripture.

The most popular Bible verse to date is John 3:16 in which Jesus, while proclaiming the gospel, instructs Nicodemus that he must be "born again". Christians have historically used this framework as the primary means by which the gospel is illustrated and shared. However, as pointed out by Jefferson Bethke in his book, "It's Not What You Think: Why Christianity Is So Much More Than Going to Heaven When You Die", Jesus only ever used that framework once in John chapter three. However, when you turn to John chapter four, Jesus presents the gospel to a woman in Samaria and does not mention being born again at all. Instead he frames the gospel in the idea of thirst and satisfaction thereby offering himself as the "living water". In John 6 he frames the gospel in the idea of hunger and introduces himself as "the bread of life." In John 10, he is the good shepherd. And so on and so forth.

The point is, Jesus is preaching the gospel in each case, but he is changing the framework. To a religious Jew who believed his natural birth was sufficient for salvation, he stresses being "born again". To a lonely woman, searching for satisfaction, he is "living water." To a crowd of hungry seekers, he becomes "the bread of life" and later on, the "good shepherd". But what happened to the "born again" metaphor? Why didn't he just stick to that one? After all, it captures the essence of salvation as being both a justifying and sanctifying act. Why risk losing that essence by using any other framework? To make matters worse, don't the other frameworks lend themselves to a consumerist approach to the gospel in which Jesus is embraced because he offers satisfaction of some sort without any inkling of individual death and rebirth? And yet, never again is Jesus recorded using that one framework. Instead, he continually reframes the gospel to meet the people where they are.

Paul did the same. When speaking to the Jews he used the Old Testament, but when speaking to the

Greeks he reframed the gospel message in their own cosmology going so far as to equate Jesus with their "unknown God" (Acts 17:23). This pattern of reframing the gospel in Jesus and Paul is nothing more than connecting the secondary ideas the gospel introduces to the primary ideas the audience was already interacting with. And because primary ideas differ from place to place, Jesus and Paul both adapted the secondary idea of the gospel to speak directly to the primary ideas of their listeners. This is the key to relevance. Paul expressed this brilliantly when he wrote:

> To the Jews I became as a Jew, that I might gain Jews; to those who are under the law, as under the law, that I might gain those who are under the law; to those who are without law, as without law (not being without law toward God, but under law toward Christ), that I might win those who are without law. To the weak I became as weak, that I might gain the weak. I have become all things to all men, that I may by all means save some. (1 Cor. 9:20-22)

However, what Jesus and Paul never did was *redefine* the gospel. Reframing is one thing. Redefining is another thing altogether. Both Jesus and Paul clearly reframed their message, but the foundation of that message was always the same. As a result, they built diverse frameworks on the solid foundation of the one gospel. Thus, Paul could say, "...even though we, or an angel from heaven, should preach to you any 'good news' other than that which we preached to you, let him be cursed." (Galatians 1:8) while simultaneously presenting that one gospel in a diversity of frameworks. Likewise, I propose that in order for the PAIJ to offer something of meaning new frameworks for interacting with it must be erected, but these new frameworks must be built on its historic foundation. Therefore, as I work my way toward that reframe let us revisit its historic foundation.

The PAIJ as We Know It

The PAIJ as we currently know it is a very religious concept that speaks value into religio-centric discussions. On its onset, it was a doctrine that helped make sense of the Great Disappointment of October 22, 1844. However, the doctrine quickly expanded to much more than just a moment in historic time. Rather, the doctrine claimed a central space in the church's understanding over three things: theodicy (which Adventists refer to as the Great Controversy), the gospel and end time events.

In relation to theodicy, the doctrine helps us conceptualize God's moral government (a concern of

Arminian-Wesleyan theology) in a way previously undone via the transparency motif. In relation to the gospel, the doctrine helps us make sense of the endless debate between Calvinism, Arminianism and the proponents of eternal security (once-saved-always-saved). By exploring the process of salvation via the sanctuary and demonstrating that the judgment begins in the church, Adventism not only resolves many of those historic soteriological tensions but it also retains justice in that a person cannot hide their villainy and hypocrisy within the garbs of religiosity, church membership or theological technicalities (as we find in once-saved-always-saved). The eye of God scans all, the records of our lives maintained in heavens sanctuary with exact precision, and only those authentically in Christ are safe. This understanding is appalling to Calvinists and proponents of eternal security but makes perfect sense to all Arminian denominations who believe that a born again person can, indeed, be lost again.[2] Thus, in the PAIJ, the Christian is called to a Christ-centered life that avoids the traps of self-focused legalism and self-centered licentiousness.[3]

And of course, the PAIJ ties into end time events and helps us tie together the conclusion of the Great Controversy as a complete eradication of all sin. This includes necessarily a rejection of eternal hell in which sin reigns in the universe eternally. Because the PAIJ is centered on "cleansing" then, the most natural direction for scripture and Adventist theology is to hold a cleansed-universe theme in which sin and sinners are no more. Hence, there can be no eternal realm in which the sin-infected souls of the rebellious damned dwell forever.

When it comes to the personal experience of the Adventist this doctrine, at best, encourages the believer to be in Christ. Self and world are forsaken for a thriving relationship with Jesus which results in a transformation of the character that reflects the love of God more and more. The belief that the judgment is now underway, and that this judgment is illustrated in the sanctuary's final cleansing ritual, shows us that God is now doing his final work on behalf of the human race. This means that, while we don't know when that work will end, the fact that he is now doing his final act to save as many as possible should motivate us to missional living.

Nevertheless, as previously mentioned, this framework tends to have value mostly in theological discussion. It also has value for a certain substrate of Adventists who have managed to comprehend the complex structure of the doctrine and, against all odds, apply it to their lives. However, enthusiastic as my description of the PAIJ above might be, the truth is very few have such an experience with it and, when it comes to those beyond our walls, the perspectives that the doctrine addresses (such as the systematic tensions between Arminian, Calvinist and OSAS soteriology) are too academic and difficult to grasp - let alone apply. Therefore, if we want the doctrine to speak value to our church and humanity as a whole, it must transcend its historic formulation.[4] Thus, for the remainder of this article I will present a possible reframing of the doctrine that addresses a universal primary idea, can be explained with a simple mechanism, and has applicatory power.[5]

Reframing the PAIJ in the Universal Primary Idea of Suffering

As we begin, I would like to suggest that one universal primary idea that is contextual to Daniel 8:14 is the idea of suffering. This idea is both meaningful to the human experience and contextual to the PAIJ. Thus, if we generate a first layer approach to the PAIJ using the framework of suffering, we will have met the main requirement for relevance - interaction with a universal primary idea - without twisting the doctrine into something it is not. Allow me to explain.

The book of Daniel, much like Revelation, is a book steeped in suffering. Not only has Israel been subjected to decades of social injustice due to its long lineage of self-absorbed governmental corruption, but it has now been conquered, ransacked and exiled by the beastly empire of Babylon.[6] Chapter one introduces us to the aftermath of this agonizing subjugation followed by the Babylonian attempt at re-education - a method of brainwashing conquered subjects in order to override their national and religious allegiances.

Sadly, Adventists - I observe - tend to interpret the book of Daniel from a position of Western privilege. We do not know the agony of suffering Daniel is acquainted with, so we don't even recognise it happening all around him. We seldom, if ever, stop to analyse the loneliness, hopelessness and anger Daniel would have experienced. The deep searching questions, the trauma of being uprooted from his homeland, of losing his autonomy and familiar environment while being forcefully thrust into a pagan society. How many sleepless nights would he have experienced? What of the death of his loved ones? Or the agony of seeing his countrymen turn their backs on God even more in order to fit into Babylonian culture? Would that have induced anxiety? Disappointment? Confusion? But it's not just experiences of suffering popping in and out of Daniel's story that I am referring to, but to the very real stream of suffering that he found himself in - a system in which the threat of death loomed daily and potentially accompanied by the post-traumatic stress induced by the constant fear of what is to come. Grant it, Daniels faith was strong, and it helped him to endure with faithfulness. But to assume that his faith made him immune to suffering and doubt is an assumption that would betray our own inexperience with the true depths of the agony of being. Thus, in our preaching on the book the impact and state of suffering is hardly explored. This separation from suffering is a gap we must work to close for it misses one of the keys to finding utility in the book - suffering and its immeasurable psychological, sociological and existential impact on the human will.

To be is to suffer. This is not the way things were designed but is certainly the way things are. The Buddha captured this well when he said, "Birth is suffering; aging is suffering; sickness is suffering; death is suffering; sorrow and lamentation, pain, grief, and despair are suffering..."[7] Friedrich Nietzsche summarised it with four words: "To live is to suffer..."[8] - a perspective echoed by holocaust survivor and author of "Man's Search for Meaning" - Viktor Frankl - when he stated that "suffering is an ineradicable part of life"[9] and the entertainer Woody Allen who captured it's essence when he wrote, "Life is full of misery, loneliness, and suffering - and it's all over much too soon."[10]

Now of course, as Christians our perspective of suffering is not as pessimistic as the world. To the contrary, suffering for the believer is filtered through the enthusiastic promise of redemption. In this sense, we find ourselves in agreement with German national and victim of Nazi ideology Anne Frank when she wrote,

> It's utterly impossible for me to build my life on a foundation of chaos, suffering and death. I see the world being slowly transformed into a wilderness; I hear the approaching thunder that, one day, will destroy us too. I feel the suffering of millions. And yet, when I look up at the sky, I somehow feel that everything will change for the better, that this cruelty too shall end, that peace and tranquility will return once more.[11]

This hope of a universe in which all is made right, in which harmony is restored and sin abolished is the foundation for how Christians, in contrast with other perspectives, interact with suffering. Despite the difference in filter though, the point remains that suffering is a universal primary idea that all are acquainted with and which the Bible does not shy away from. Hence, the narrative of scripture is a tale of paradise lost, followed by the agony of shame, relational breakdown and pain in labor and childbirth. The people of Israel suffered. The heroes of Israel suffered. Jesus himself was made "perfect through sufferings" (Hebrews 2:10) and indeed endured the greatest of all human sufferings by tasting not only his own immediate suffering, but the suffering of all humanity (Hebrews 2:9) - a suffering induced by separation from God (Matthew 27:46). And nowhere in scripture are we promised a reprieve from suffering. To the contrary we are promised an extra measure of it (John 15:20). Therefore, life and existence are intertwined with the state of suffering.

But it's more insidious than that. Suffering is not just something that *is* but something that *is perpetuated*. And the most damning part of the entire thing is that this state of suffering we despise is perpetuated by our very own human will. That is, suffering continues to spread, expand and demolish because it has a host through which it can self-perpetuate - the human heart. And this host, unified into empire, becomes a beast that devours, tramples and crushes (Daniel 7). Thus, in the end suffering is more than just something we experience but something we prolong. That is, we are the nurturers, perpetrators and apparent immortalizers of suffering.

Driven by the impulse of self, human beings cannot help but perpetuate suffering in some way at some stage in their life. Consequently, it is not simply true that we live because Christ died, but that Christ died because we live. Our very being demanded a sacrifice before it was actuated (Revelation 13:8) due to the risk and eventual manifestation of human selfishness. And it is from this obsession and impulse of the self that suffering continues to dominate the human story. The Dalai Lama expressed this well when he said that, "The extreme self-centered attitude is the source of suffering."[12] The journalist Dennis Prager also captured this reality when he wrote,

> There is no limit to suffering human beings have been willing to inflict on others, no matter how innocent, no matter how young, and no matter how old. This fact must lead all reasonable human beings, that is, all human beings who take evidence seriously, to draw only one possible conclusion: Human nature is not basically good.[13]

Take this individual reality and multiply it by millions of people, and you end up with the "beasts" of Daniel 7. They are beasts because human empire is nothing more than a collective self that is driven by the impulse of self, resulting in the perpetuation of suffering on a grandeur, more systemic scale. Sadly, in the West, society is plastic. We live in an artificial, matrix-like version of reality, in which our consciousness is plugged into a veneer of endless diversion, amusements and social currencies. Thus, professor Cedric Vine could say that in the West, Christian worship is the worship of thankfulness for prosperity whereas outside the West, Christian worship is the worship of lamentation.[14] Because of this, we seem to miss the presence of suffering in Daniel even though its embedded in the text all the way up to the age of the church. But if we find it and extrapolate it from the text, it can lead us to a framework for teaching Daniel - including Daniel 8:14 and its resulting PAIJ - in a way that speaks to the universal primary idea of suffering without having to force fit suffering into the doctrines scope of vision.

How does it work?

But how exactly does this "suffering-reframe" thing work? It's really quite simple. Within this experience of suffering we encounter Daniel, a Jewish-teenage captive immersed in a struggle between two kingdoms. This two-kingdom tension is everywhere in Daniels book and pictures the kingdom of God in a historic struggle with the kingdom of man. There is a pattern here that cannot be ignored. A tension between two kingdoms is repeated over and over again, and beneath this cosmic struggle lies the very real effect of collateral human suffering.

Chapter seven keeps the same pattern of war between two kingdoms. We are taken on a vision of human and divine struggle culminating in the injustice of the church, its perpetuation of suffering and ultimately, its judgment which ends with the kingdom of God declared sovereign over the earth. This is the same pattern as the previous chapters: a struggle between two kingdoms resulting in the suffering of the innocent and culminating in the annihilation of human empire which is then replaced by the eternal kingdom. Finally, we arrive at chapter eight in which we are once again shown a more detailed vision of the events. The battle between two kingdoms is pictured again, followed by the perpetuation of suffering, and reaches its apex in the injustice of the church which is consequently destroyed. The PAIJ finds itself smack in the middle of all of this and, if framed in the common experience of suffering, it will speak to human needs in a way our present formulations often fail to do.

Transition 1

At this point, everything we have explored interacts with the universal primary idea of suffering, and its derived primary ideas of injustice and the struggle between good and evil. Each of these themes are felt and discussed everywhere from Hollywood's "Marvel Cinematic Universe" to the mythological narratives of unreached tribal nations. Daniel's visions speak directly to these universal primary ideas by acknowledging not only their existence but also exposing the thing which perpetuates them - human empire driven by human will. In doing so, Daniel's vision sets the foundation for introducing a kingdom made "without hands" (Daniel 2:34) which conquers the whole earth and dwells forever in justice and love.[15]

So far, we have merely set the foundation for reframing the PAIJ. Rather than looking at Daniel from a religio-centric perspective, we can see that it interacts with the universal human question of suffering. By acquainting ourselves with suffering, both individual and systemic, we can capture the relevance inherent in the book and speak value to the human experience. However, we are not done. To truly reframe the PAIJ we must also embrace simplicity. I would like to introduce this simplicity by zooming in on the PAIJ itself introduced in chapter eight.

Here we are shown that Satan's entire campaign has a target. He climbs to the height of power and, once there, he attacks the sanctuary. If we are to picture the history of human empire as repeated experiments in the war against God, then the church emerges as Satan's latest and best invention. All of the anomalies have been removed. And now, with his greatest weapon he goes to war against God by "cast[ing] down" (Daniel 8:11) his sanctuary. But why? And what does this ancient and forgotten cultic edifice have to do with the universal primary idea of suffering?

At this point I want to step away from the first element of the PAIJ's rebirth (connecting it to a universal primary idea) and into the second element - simplifying its mechanics so that even a child can comprehend the narrative.

Simplifying the Mechanics of the PAIJ

This is the point in the visions in which we, as Adventists, have a big decision to make. Will we continue here to speak to universal primary ideas? Or will we shift gears and turn to religio-centric concerns that have little meaning outside of our Adventist box? Historically speaking, that is precisely what we have done. Once we arrive at the sanctuary in Daniel, we dive into a detailed and exhausting investigation on the sanctuary and arrive at conclusions so complicated few people can keep up (and fewer still find interesting). I would like to propose that, while those detailed investigations have some value, they are not necessary for the culture to gain a proper grasp of the visions thematic aim and are, in fact, counterproductive. The sanctuary in scripture simply represents two things. First, God's desire to dwell with his people (Exodus 25:8) and second, God's plan to bring us back into that "dwelling" (the gospel, John 1:29). There is no need to make it more complicated than that.

Thus, the sanctuary which represents God's "withness" emerges in chapter eight as a primary target of the enemy and when we cast a bird's eye view over scriptures narrative, we can see this tension over the sanctuary everywhere. But the question we are interested in is why? Why is Satan so bent on destroying the sanctuary? The answer is simple. If the sanctuary represents God's connection with humanity, then it's "casting down" represents an attempt at damaging that connection. In other words, the sanctuary represents God's "withness", but Satan is bent on our separation. Thus, he attacks the sanctuary in order to secure separation between us and God.[16] He tramples on the gospel so that he can keep his prisoners, locked safely in the ideological prison of his own making, a prison built on the idea that God is separated from us. Therefore, Satan aims to trample the gospel (sanctuary) because it is in the gospel that man and God are reconciled. He wants to bring separation. And all the war and suffering in the human story are simply collateral effects of Satan's campaign toward divine-human separation.[17]

This concept is very simple to grasp. There is no need to go into Leviticus and explore Yom Kippur or the entirety of the sanctuary services. These can be explored at a later time in the third layer of depth. But here, in the first layer, we simply look at the battle between two kingdoms. Man's kingdom, undergirded by Satan, and God's kingdom represented by Christ. Satan works to separate us from God (casts down the sanctuary) and God works to end the separation (restoration of the sanctuary). And in that tension between withness and separation lies the experience of suffering. Suffering is not simply pain, misfortune or oppression - suffering is separation. And in a collective, global sense Satan systematized this separation into the universal church depicted as an "other horn" in Daniel 7. The suffering now self-perpetuates through the automated funnel of religious influence. Is there no end in sight?

Keeping it Simple in Daniel 8: 13-14

We finally arrive at Daniel 8:13 in which a being in the vision asks the question, "How long will the vision about the continual burnt offering, and the disobedience that makes desolate, to give both the sanctuary and the army to be trodden under foot be?"

The language in this question alone is confusing but if we slow down, we will find it is simple. There is an attack against God centered on his sanctuary. The heavenly being wants to know how long the continual sacrifice (gospel) will be "[taken] away" (Daniel 8:11), how long the disobedience that makes desolate (war, devastation, ruin) will go on and how long the sanctuary and God's people will be trampled. "How long?" is the basic question.

But let us linger there for a moment for the question itself is not exclusively theological. Rather, it is an utterance emerging from suffering. How long until...? Is the kind of question you ask when your present experience is no longer desirable. How long until lunch? Is asked when the present reality of hunger pangs has reached a torturous point. How long until vacation? Is asked when the present demands of work have peaked your stress levels. But the question does not simply denote exhaustion with a present, menial experience but with agonizing imprisonment from which there seems to be no reprise. How long? is the kind of question one would expect a slave, after years of working the fields like an ox, to whisper as he lies down at night, his back reshaped by the scars of the master's whip. It is the question asked by a child immersed in the darkness of cyberbullying before sinking into suicidal despair, of a woman whose entire family has been massacred by war or genocide.

How long? is the cry emanating from the halls of Auschwitz, from the souls of the sex-slaves bound to underground brothels, and from the mother who buried her child in the aftermath of yet another mass shooting. How long? is the cry of martyred souls who beckon to heaven, "How long, Master, the holy and true, until you judge and avenge our blood on those who dwell on the earth?" (Revelation 6:10). It is the utterance from the lips of a prophet who, despairing of life cried out, "[H]ow long will I cry, and you will not hear? I cry out to you 'Violence!' and will you not save?" (Habakkuk 1:2). How long can the human heart endure such agony? How long until the pain outweighs any justification we concoct for our existence? It's the cry of the dispossessed, the ostracized, the outcast who cannot fathom taking another breath. The cry of the abused and mistreated. The question ought to make us weep. It is a question that is sacred. It treads on the ground of agony, of human tears and mortal blood. How long?

But the question is more than an echo of human suffering. It is also a question that peels back the layers of alter-dimensional reality and helps us glimpse, even if for a moment, the parallel suffering of heaven. Its inhabitants are not disconnected. The question of suffering haunts angelic society as much as that of men. Looking upon the events of the vision - the war against the sanctuary with its resulting perpetuation of human suffering - one being in heaven despairs of the pain. Seldom do we stop to ponder angelic suffering. This being has been at the center of the struggle. He has witnessed his companions join Satan in the rebellion. He carries the trauma of desolation, of witnessing the dark depths to which humanity can sink, of Satan inspiring the most grotesque expressions of worship as men sacrificed their own children in fire. But worst of all, he has witnessed the violent murder of heavens prince. The being has beheld his share of suffering. And now, with the gospel plan accomplished, he longs for an end to the separation and the suffering. But there doesn't seem to be an end in sight. The other horn wages war and succeeds. The sanctuary is cast down. The people of God become objects of vengeful intolerance. The world seems darker than ever before. "How long?" The angel blurts out. "Until the vision is fulfilled?" (*NIV*)

I would like to remind the reader, at this juncture, that I am not here dealing with theological or systematic validity. I am dealing with doctrinal utility. And to that end I would say, Adventism must derive its identity not from Daniel 8:14 alone but from Daniel 8:13. Verse 14 gives us the answer to the question, but verse 13 gives us the question. Sadly, Adventism is a movement that rushes to answers. Afterall, our identity is rooted in an answer, so it makes sense. Our evangelism is all about answers. Our Bible studies are all about answers. Our witnessing is about answers. Oh, that we would someday forsake our obsession with answers just long enough to sit with the question! Daniel 8:13 must become a part of our identity. We must identify with the suffering. But you cannot do so if you rush to ponder, pontificate and philosophize. You can only do so if you sit with the question, with the suffering, and simply breathe.

Allow me to summarize my point so far. Do you want the PAIJ to have utility for the human experience? Here is my plain suggestion: *It must be reframed in suffering.*

Suffering is the context of Daniel. It is the context of Revelation. Both were written in exile. Both were written far from home. Both were written with a longing to be home. Both were written by a displaced, ostracized and outcast people. A people suffering. A people facing political and literal extinction at nearly every turn - the Jews in Persia, the Christians in Rome. The visions are bathed and immersed in struggle, in agony, in pain. War tugs at each text, two kingdoms locked in a cosmic conflict over the souls of men. And the enemy of men and God tramples on his sanctuary with one objective - to separate man from God forever. To immerse us in terminal cancerous suffering and a hopeless nihilistic fate that would strangle our very will to exist.

Transition 2

So, what exactly have I proposed so far? It's really quite simple. In order for the doctrine of the PAIJ to have meaning for the culture, we must connect it to a universal primary idea. I propose that the experience of suffering is a perfect fit. However, we must also teach it with greater simplicity. By focusing on the broad themes of the sanctuary and leaving the other more detailed elements for deeper study at a later time, we can give people not only a doctrine that interacts with a very real human need but do so in a way that doesn't require people to sit through complex and overwhelming charts and diagrams. We will explore this more in the next installment of the series.

In short, the framework above is simple. All you are really doing is telling a story of war resulting in suffering to which God promises a reversal. That is basically it. It doesn't have to be more complicated than that. By doing so, the doctrine is introduced in a way that both connects to a universal primary idea and has a simple mechanics that can be followed even by a child.

However, one more element remains before we can truly say we have achieved a relevant conceptualisation of the PAIJ. That element is what I refer to as "applicatory power". This is the part in which we ask, what difference does this make? And this is perhaps the most important and forgotten portion of the doctrine. While some Adventists have managed to see the PAIJ in a meaningful way and also understand it within its traditional framework, fewer still are able to answer the question - so what? What difference does it make? It is to this final element that we now turn.

Discovering the PAIJ's Applicatory Power

The visions of Daniel are a narrative of struggle between two kingdoms. The struggle is marked by collateral suffering. This suffering is the result of separation from God. Even heaven despairs with the question, "How long?" To which an answer is given: "It will take 2,300 evenings and mornings; then the sanctuary will be reconsecrated." (Daniel 8:14) The answer has many layers of depth to it, but if we stick to the first layer it simply means this: The separation Satan is working to induce will not succeed. The sanctuary will be restored. God will reverse the evil of empire.

But the restoration of the sanctuary is a historical process, not a moment in time. This means that before Jesus returns, God is engaged in the process of restoring his connection and his gospel to all humanity. This reality is reflected in Ellen White's prediction that "the final message to be given to this world will be a revelation of God's character of love."[18] For centuries Satan labored to darken the earth. But a line was drawn in the sand and God declared, no more. And thus, began the PAIJ, as the beginning of the end of suffering. The tribunal for universal social justice convened on that day and is soon to close. The judgment is here. Separation is being erased. Suffering is being erased. The gospel is not just a message of forgiveness and future hope for salvation. The gospel is a message of restoration to God's original design. And this restoration involves the very annihilation of suffering. God is not simply introducing a new kingdom; he is reversing the effects of the old.[19]

When asked about suffering, the Buddha concluded that it was the result of desire that could only be escaped when one overcame desire itself. Others proposed suffering was a mere illusion. To the Hindus it is karma and exacerbated by "past inappropriate action".[20] To the Jews it is encapsulated in a reward and punishment system among various other theories.[21] To the Muslim it is intended to identify the righteous and caused by un-submission to Allah.[22] To the Baha'i it is a stage in our spiritual evolution.[23] To the classical Christian it is an anomaly to be fixed at the return of Jesus. To the gospel narrative however, suffering is more than a state but a condition of being to be healed. This perspective is amplified by the PAIJ which sees human will as the perpetuator of suffering which will cease by healing, or "reversing" the impulse of self within the human heart and restore humanity to the impulse of love.

In this sense, the PAIJ is not simply God reversing suffering but reversing the perpetuation of suffering. However, this does not take place through human legislation or political science as the social justice warriors and evangelicals of the day insist - rather it takes place through the gospel reversing the impulse of self in the human heart. In order for suffering to end, the human heart must be healed of the beastly drive toward self-promotion and returned to the heavenly design of selfless love. In our traditional conceptualisation of the PAIJ, we tend to view the cleansing of the sanctuary primarily as a legal act in which God is removing data of sins committed from the sanctuary in heaven. Without denying this, the present framework emphasizes the experiential cleansing over the legal. That is, God is removing the impulse of self from the human heart rather than simply cleaning up a ledger in heaven. God engages in this process of reversal in heavens sanctuary by reversing the work of evil (perpetuated by the church, human empire and human impulse). All of us are invited to allow God, through his grace, to reverse the impulse of self within and replace it with the design of love.

Ellen White expressed this angle of the PAIJ well when commenting on Jesus' cleansing of the earthly temple. She writes,

> In cleansing the temple from the world's buyers and sellers, Jesus announced His mission to cleanse the heart from the defilement of sin, — from the earthly desires, the selfish lusts, the evil habits, that corrupt the soul.[24]

These earthly desires are the impulse of self through which suffering perpetuates both individually and, more tragically, systemically when the impulse is institutionalized via the power of empire and church. Thus, for Adventists, the reversal of suffering is not to be found in policies, institutions or governmental structures but in the gospels power to reverse the impulse of self and restore the human heart to the design of love.

This restoration, however, must move us to pour out onto the earth with a heart for the suffering. To quote Nathan Brown, we must become "agents of reversal"[25] in our world. In light of a present judgment in which suffering and the perpetuation of suffering via man made systems and empires are being undone, we discover applicatory power that invites all who embrace this message to be part of the reversal. It is this call to be "agents of reversal" bolstered by the reality of a present judgment in which the reversal is already underway that can provide the PAIJ with applicatory power and likewise, redefine the identity of Adventism as a movement.

Why? Because our message is not simply one of forgiveness and reconciliation or legal justification or philosophical apologetics. Our message is one for the suffering. Adventism is a church for the suffering. Our evangelism is a message for the suffering. The PAIJ gives us a vision of the existential divine-human separation as coming to an end in the present flow of history. Since the judgment began in 1844, suffering is reversing via the restoration of divine-human connection through the gospel and its transformative effect - a gospel that was trampled and distorted through the decades of counter-narrative promulgated by the institutional church. This element of the gospel places it beyond mere legal amendments and into the human heart. The result is that through his grace, God heals his people from self-centered perpetrators of suffering, to other centered reversers of suffering. Consequently, we no longer fit into human empire. We become wanderers on the earth driven by a kingdom ethic of love rather than the beastly impulse of self. Therefore, Adventists above all people, should be active in sitting with the suffering, raging against the systems of suffering and preparing society for a world inhabited by those who have forsaken the impulse of self that leads to suffering.

Interestingly, it is the reversal of suffering that inspired the pioneers to join the prohibition movement.[26] They were not fundamentalists who hated alcohol because they found a Bible verse that said, "alcohol bad". Rather, they saw alcohol as a social ill that fueled interpersonal, societal and national suffering. On top of this, they saw that alcohol always had an adverse effect in poorer communities. It broke down the family unit, parental responsibility and economic stability resulting in the abuse of wives and children. Thus, alcohol did not simply inebriate the cognitive sensibilities but was part of the system that led to socio-economic, developmental and relational suffering especially among poorer communities who could hardly recover from its effects. Thus, to oppose alcohol for our pioneers was akin to opposing the perpetuation of suffering.[27] This same perspective led

Ellen White to recommend Adventists to vote for prohibition even on the Sabbath and also led her to command civil disobedience to the church rather than return a slave to its owner[28] and undergirded the health message and its positive impact on reversing the curse of disease which had, to a large degree, become the cultural norm.[29]

Tragically, the reversal of suffering motif seems to have died with our pioneers. Following after them, the church has not done a good job at maintaining this vision. Had we done so, what would Adventism have been during the Jim Crow era?[30] Would Lucy Byard have died on the steps of an Adventist hospital that refused to admit her simply for being black?[31] Would mainstream German Adventist Churches have echoed hatred of Jews and become instruments for the perpetuation of suffering ushered in by the Third Reich?[32] Would the first clergy man sentenced for war crimes in Rwanda have been an ordained Seventh-day Adventist minister?[33] What would have been our message to a world frightened by the threat of communism and nuclear annihilation? And what of the present context of fear driven by our erratic political climate?

We can only speculate, but my belief is that, had we reframed our doctrine in suffering rather than constraining it to parameters that had long lost their significance for us, our history would be different. Imagine Adventists living in society by self-identifying as "agents of reversal" in their neighborhoods, workplaces and families? How would our local churches function if we saw them as "spaces of reversal" in their communities? How would our pastors and conferences prioritize and strategize if the leaders saw themselves as "delegates of reversal" in their regions? How would our personal spiritual lives be impacted if we daily sought to allow grace to reverse the impulse of self within each of us? An impulse that breeds suffering whenever it is exercised.

Instead, our identifying doctrine - the PAIJ - has been reduced to a mere religious formula that raises debates and arguments only hyper-religious theological nerds find interesting. Consequently, our youth find the doctrine meaningless.[34] Our local churches have zero impact on their local communities and our history is filled with the very perpetuation of suffering that the PAIJ promises to undo. We have gotten locked in an outdated framework that has kept us disconnected from society, lost in endless theological banter, while the world outside oscillates between hope and despair with naught a word from the one movement that claims to be the present truth for the final days.

Conclusion

My invitation is this - let us not discount the frameworks of old but let us build on them by finding exactly where the PAIJ belongs. And it belongs in the center of suffering. It must be framed in suffering. Understood in suffering. Expressed in suffering and beheld in suffering. For it is a doctrine that emerges in the context of suffering and challenges us to become agents of reversal in the midst of suffering - a church working to reverse the suffering perpetuated by the governmental systems of man's beastly empire through the power of the gospel and active, humanitarian involvement in our communities.

The combination of Arminian theology, the Great Controversy motif, our apocalyptic consciousness, Christ-centered vision and the Pre-Advent Investigative Judgment narrative provides Adventism with the raw materials to be the most powerful, satisfying and meaningful voice on the universal primary idea of suffering. But in order for us to finally occupy that space in the culture, we must reframe our conceptualisation and application of the PAIJ from religio-centric to a voice for the suffering that sits with both the idea of suffering and its contemporary, systemic expression. As the philosopher Nietzsche implied, we must - like a snake

- shed our skin or risk death itself. And if we do, the sanctuary can once again become a unifying element of Adventist theology that strings our entire message together into a cohesive story that will speak value to humanity. If it was able to do so during a time when our audience was primarily Christian and engaged in traditional theological considerations, why can't it do it again in our contemporary secular age? The only variable to decide this is us.

As I close this article, you might find yourself with some large questions such as, How does reframing the PAIJ in suffering interact with the doctrines historic priorities? Does this reframe somehow damage our apocalyptic warning to the world? Can this reframe prepare society for the deceptions soon to come upon it? These and other questions will be answered in the next two articles in the series in which I close with an overview on how we can easily and accurately teach this perspective of the PAIJ in a way that not only addresses the universal primary concern of suffering, but also provide a solid foundation for a person's theological foundations.

Chapter Summary

- Reframing a doctrine is not simply biblically permissible, but theologically required. Jesus and his apostles often reframed their message in order to interact with the diverse ideas and experiences of their listeners.

- One textually sound and meaningful concept in which to reframe the PAIJ is the concept of universal suffering. By reframing the PAIJ as part of the divine response to judgment, the doctrine gains a new level of synthesis with the rest of scriptures narrative and becomes meaningful to the contemporary, post-church mind.

- Reframing the PAIJ in the concept of suffering is not mere semantical novelty. Rather, it aims to redefine our identity, priorities and lifestyles as Seventh-day Adventists. As a result, the doctrine emerges with an applicatory power our traditional frameworks have always lacked.

Discussion Questions

1. What do you think about the way Jesus and his apostles reframed their message? And why are we, in modern Adventism, so resistant to do the same?

2. Share your thoughts on reframing the PAIJ to speak meaningfully to the universal primary idea of suffering. What is your reaction to this reframe?

3. How do you feel about the call to be "agents of reversal" in our communities and spheres of influence? Can you see how this reframe, if properly navigated, can inspire us to embrace God's mission in the world with greater clarity and energy? Also, how does it impact your own personal faith expression?

Chapter Endnotes

1. When I speak of the validity of our historic understanding, I do not refer to the doctrine's corruption via frameworks like perfectionism and Last Generation Theology. I contend that these systems of thought are not only heretical but are highly to blame for the doctrines contemporary demise.

2. For more see Manea, Mike & Marcos Torres. "Why the Critics of the Investigative Judgment Have Failed," [Web: https://thecompassmagazine.com/blog/why-the-critics-of-the-investigative-judgment-have-failed] and Manea, Mike. "How Adventism Ended the Gospel Wars," [Web: https://thecompassmagazine.com/blog/how-adventism-ended-the-gospel-wars]

3. For more see, Torres, Marcos D. "Facing Life's Record: An Analysis of The Great Controversy's Scariest Chapter," [Web: https://thestorychurchproject.com/bloghost//2013/08/facing-lifes-record-analysis-of-great.html]

4. However, certain rules must be in place. The first I have already mentioned - that a reframing of the PAIJ must build on its foundation and not deconstruct it. The second is that the reframing cannot be forced. That is, we cannot simply look at the needs of humanity and then twist the PAIJ, like a pretzel to try

and make it fit somewhere. A better alternative to fitting in, argues social worker Brené Brown, is "belonging". And while she is addressing intrapersonal concerns and not ideological ones, this perspective can nevertheless be appropriated for our present task. Thus, I contend that rather than trying to make the PAIJ fit in with modern culture we must, instead, discover where it naturally belongs in the realm of universal primary ideas. In this way, we can arrive at an authentic reframing and avoid disingenuous formulations in the name of "relevance". The third is that reframing the PAIJ must, of necessity, provide us with a simple message that can be understood by all. This does not mean the task of reframing is simplistic. As will be seen in the remainder of this article, there is a lot of work to do there. In fact, this entire article series calling for a reframing is itself moderately complex. What we need, however, is to translate that process into a simple message that can be presented without demanding a prerequisite of theological education or immersing into doctrinal mechanics that people struggle to comprehend. For more in the difference between fitting in and belonging see CBS News. "Author Brené Brown on the difference between belonging and fitting in," [Web: https://www.cbsnews.com/news/author-brene-brown-social-scientist-new-book-braving-the-wilderness]

5. The final point to also keep in mind is that reframing the PAIJ is not about finding a new framework by which we constrict the doctrine all over again. If the foundation is properly set, then reframing the PAIJ is about discovering a diversity of ways, or a continuum of frames, in which the doctrine can be expressed and communicated. In this present article I offer one framework, but I contend that other frameworks relevant to diverse audiences can and must be found. I leave that task up to other thinkers to explore.

6. This is witnessed in chapter one with the struggle between Babylon and Israel functioning as a microcosm of the war between Christ and Satan. The tension is repeated in chapter two with the story of human empire being ground to powder by the invading eternal kingdom, in chapter three with the battle over worship, in chapter four with God's judgment over Nebuchadnezzar, in chapter five with Belshazzar taunting God and in chapter six with another struggle over worship, Daniel on death-row, and the Median King ultimately submitting to God's kingdom.

7. New World Encyclopedia. "Suffering," [Web: http://www.newworldencyclopedia.org/entry/Suffering]

8. As quoted in, Wachs, Stephanie W. "On Survival (Or To Live Is To Suffer)," [Web:

https://medium.com/@stephaniewittelswachs/on-survival-or-to-live-is-to-suffer-857749f9c66e]

9. Frankl, Viktor Emil and William J. Winslade. "Man's Search for Meaning"

10. As quoted in, Johnston, Janis C., "Midlife Maze: A Map to Recovery and Rediscovery after Loss," p. 91.

11. Anne Frank House. "A choir of voices: Holocaust diaries by Anne Frank and other young writers," [Web: https://www.annefrank.org/en/anne-frank/go-in-depth/holocaust-diaries-anne-frank-and-other-young-writer]

12. Karl, Jonathan, Richard Coolidge and Jordyn Phelps "The Dalai Lama's secret to happiness in 140 characters," [Web: https://news.yahoo.com/blogs/power-players-abc-news/the-dalai-lamas-secret-to-happiness-in-140-characters-191833143.html]

13. Prager, Dennis. "A Letter from Africa," [Web: https://www.dennisprager.com/letter-africa]

14. Advent Next Podcast. "Faith and Politics from the Gospel of Matthew - Dr Cedric Vine," ep. 2 [Web: https://www.adventnext.com/podcasts]

15. Now of course, one can just as easily look at the book of Daniel and say that the struggle between the two kingdoms is a struggle over the truth of God's character versus lies. This is an alternate framework to suffering through which the entire narrative can be contextualised as well. Or we can frame the visions in judgment which is also a recurring theme in the

entire book and a primary idea most people are familiar with. It can be framed in government, political science, world religion, the gospel - even mental health! My point by focusing on suffering is not that it is the only way of introducing the PAIJ to the culture, but that it is one potential framework that can be used to contextualise the doctrine in the language and concerns that people are actually talking about.

16. This attack on the sanctuary is not new. When Babylon conquered Israel it destroyed the earthly sanctuary. Then, under Medo-Persian rule God delivered his people back to Israel to rebuild it. Satan attempted, over and over again, to prevent its reconstruction but he failed. Two entire books in the OT are dedicated to this rebuilding: Ezra and Nehemiah. Next, the Greek empire swept through and the sanctuary was once again attacked. Antiochus Epiphanes comes to mind as one of the most anti-sanctuary figures during that time. But Antiochus is but a small player in a much larger narrative. By the time Jesus arrives, Rome is the new empire in town. It subjugates the Jews and offers them a puppet king named Herod. The temple is still a center for Jewish worship but has become a mere rite of ceremonies and an economic center. The place of God's meeting with man has been trampled so much that it has lost its meaning. As a result, Jesus performs a microcosm of the sanctuary's cleansing

when he lashes out against the vendors in the temple for their perpetuation of human suffering (John 2:12-22). The one place that was meant to symbolise God's connection to humanity had been transformed into a place of exploitation which gave rise to the systemic rejection of the poor. After cleansing the temple, Jesus welcomed the poor and outcasts. His judgment restored the people's connection with God via the temple. He had interrupted the perpetuation of suffering.

17. Is this all the "casting down" of the sanctuary represents? Of course not! But it's all that you need to explore in the first layer of the doctrine. You can add onto this in layers two and three. But as far as the first layer is concerned, keep it there. It's so simple even a child can grasp it and it also sets a foundation for adding more in the future.

18. White, Ellen G. "Last Day Events," p. 200

19. Jesus, as was mentioned earlier, voluntarily entered into the greatest type of suffering when he experienced separation from God on our behalf. Thus, there is a deep connection between the perpetuation of suffering and our separation from God illustrated by a trampled sanctuary.

20. Whitman, Sarah M., "Pain and Suffering as Viewed by the Hindu Religion," [Web: http://www.uphs.upenn.edu/pastoral/events/hindu_painsuffering.pdf]

21. My Jewish Learning, "Jewish Answers to Suffering and Evil," [Web: https://www.myjewishlearning.com/article/jewish-answers-to-suffering-and-evil]

22. Patheos Religion Library: Islam, "Suffering and the Problem of Evil, " [Web: https://www.patheos.com/library/islam/beliefs/suffering-and-the-problem-of-evil]

23. Oliveira, Marco. "A Starting Point for Understanding Suffering," [Web: https://bahaiteachings.org/starting-point-for-understanding-suffering]

24. White, Ellen G. "The Desire of Ages," p. 161

25. The Story Church Project. "Should Adventist Churches be Involved in Social Justice? with Nathan Brown," [Web: https://thestorychurchproject.com/bloghost/2019/3/17/should-adventist-churches-be-involved-in-social-justice-with-nathan-brown]

26. See: Miller, Jared. "Adventists, Prohibition, and Political Involvement," [Web: http://libertymagazine.org/article/adventists-prohibition-and-political-involvement]

27. Whitaker, Rachel. "Drying Up the Stream," [Web: https://www.adventistreview.org/archives/2004-1504/story1.html]

28. Branson, Roy. "Ellen G. White: Racist or Champion of Equality?", [Web:

http://www.oakwood.edu/additional_sites/goldmine/ hdoc/blacksda/champ/index.html]

29. See White, Ellen G. "Ministry of Health and Healing," and Knight, George R. "Ellen White's World."

30. Hollancid, Cleran. "'Race' and the Adventist Church," [Web: https://thecompassmagazine.com/blog/race-and-the-adventist-church]

31. North American Regional Voice. "Memories of My Grandmother, Lucille Byard," [Web: http://www.blacksdahistory.org/remembering-lucy-byard.html]

32. Schroder, Corrie. "Seventh Day Adventists," [Web: http://www.history.ucsb.edu/projects/holocaust/Rese arch/Proseminar/corrieschroder.htm?fbclid=IwAR1v OZlLvN0hy02ORDHtNcJMYYQBbvLplCsNbpN-Mlyg6dx-Jbc1U8FFi_l]

33. Carroll, Rory. "Pastor who led Tutsis to slaughter is jailed," [Web: https://www.theguardian.com/world/2003/feb/20/ror ycarroll1]

34. See both "Seventh-day Adventist Young Adult Study," Barna Group, 2013, [Web: http://www.youngadultlife.com/wp-content/uploads/2015/01/Barna-SDA-Millennials-Report-final.pdf] and "21st Century Seventh-day Adventist Connection Study," [Web: https://www.adventistarchives.org/the-twenty-%C2%AD%E2%80%90first-century-seventh-

%C2%AD%E2%80%90day-adventist-connection-
study.pdf]

5.

Reteaching the Pre-Advent Investigative Judgment

"Ever more people today have the means to
live, but no meaning to live for."

—— Victor Frankl

In the previous article, I introduced a possible
reframing of the Pre-Advent Investigative Judgment
(PAIJ). This reframe provides relevance by interacting
with the universal primary idea of suffering through a
simple explanatory mechanic that in turn produces a
perspective that has applicatory power. The
combination of these three elements, I suggested,
provides a "first layer" of depth for understanding the
PAIJ that can then be enhanced through further
study into what I referred to as the second and third
layers.

The challenge for Adventism is that we tend to
explore the doctrine at the third layer of depth from
the onset and this in turn forces us to introduce the

doctrine in a framework that is disconnected from universal primary ideas and difficult to comprehend due to its complex anatomy. This, in turn, results in the near impossibility of finding applicatory power in the doctrine as is evidenced by the high number of Seventh-day Adventists who can hardly explain it, let alone enact it in everyday life.

However, as already mentioned, this does not mean that the doctrinal formulation is wrong. It simply means it's too much too soon. The solution, therefore, is not to get rid of what we have built but to simplify it into a process of learning that ranges from the simple to the complex. In truth, every doctrine in scripture functions this way. For example, justification by faith can be explained in a few simple sentences but can also be explored in volumes ranging over 600 pages. We would never dream of using that volume while trying to reach the culture because of its complexity. Instead, we would stick to the simple models to help people grasp the core of the message to which they can build on as the years go by. Likewise, my proposal is that our current approach to the PAIJ tends itself toward the complex and must be replaced by a simpler approach which new believers can easily grasp and then add to throughout their discipleship journey in the years to come.

Thus, in this article I want to explore, in a bit more detail, what the three layers of depth can look like when teaching the PAIJ in a way that provides meaning to the culture.

The First Layer

By way of review, the first layer of the doctrine is the layer which introduces the broad themes addressed by the PAIJ. This is also the level at which we frame the concept in universal primary ideas so that our exploration remains relevant to society and culture at large. There are no charts, calculations or diagrams in this layer. In a sense, this layer is more like a story where the exploration centers on a narrative plot line of conflict, complication and resolution.

Here is a brief outline of how this approach can be explored in Bible studies or evangelistic sermons. This outline is the step by step approach that I personally use when studying the Bible with seekers and unchurched contacts:

1. Conflict: Introduce the book of Daniel as a war between two kingdoms – God's and man's - with Satan working to induce eternal separation between us and God.

2. Complication: Identify suffering as the collateral effect of this separation. This includes both the presence of suffering as well as the perpetuation of suffering via human will.

3. Resolution: Introduce the question of Daniel 8:13 in the context of suffering. Explore the sanctuary in its broad themes: "withness" of God in the gospel. It's trampling or defiling simply means God's withness and gospel (the things that reverse suffering) are under attack. This attack is led by human empire, including the church itself, and results in the perpetuation of suffering. (Avoid complicated charts and elongated explanations of furniture, architecture etc.) Daniel 8:14 then becomes a resolution to the universal primary idea of suffering. The restoration of the sanctuary can now be easily explained as a reversal of suffering, without complex deliberations on the Day of Atonement or having to go into Hebrew terminology or historical analyses (this can be reserved for future 2nd and 3rd layer studies).

As you can see, reframing the PAIJ doesn't simply impact the way we approach Daniel 8:14 but rather the way we approach our entire message to begin with. Daniel must be approached from the perspective of suffering. But more so, the Great Controversy and indeed the totality of the Adventist narrative needs to be reframed to speak life to this universal primary idea. Afterall, the PAIJ is simply one chapter in the story that is Adventist theology and it must be treated as such. If you attempt to reframe the PAIJ while leaving the rest of your theological framework untouched it won't work. But if your entire framework is redesigned to speak like to the universal primary idea of suffering and separation, then reteaching the PAIJ becomes a surprisingly simple task.

About a week ago, I met with one of the secular contacts I have been studying the Bible with throughout the year. He is a young man who recently got out of rehab for drug addiction. During the previous year, many Christians have poured into him and tried to help him understand the message of scripture using old, religio-centric frameworks. This young man has been so weirded out and overwhelmed that he told me he was about ready to give up on the entire faith thing. During the time we were together I explained the message of Adventism to him using the framework of suffering and its applicatory call for God's people to be agents of reversal during the judgment phase of the redemption story. His eyes shot open. "Well, when you put it like that it makes total sense!" He said. "People have been telling me God is going to use me to be an evangelist, spread his word, cast out demons etc. and I always reply, 'Nah man, that's not for me' because it makes no sense to me. But if you are telling me that what God actually wants is to turn me into an agent of reversal that perpetuates love in the world instead of selfishness, I can totally get down with that!"

We have yet to discuss Yom Kippur, the sanctuary rituals, furniture or any of the other complex elements Adventists often bring to the table in this study but already he is excited about the thing that matters most - God's desire to metamorph a drug addict into an agent of his love in the world. That's what the PAIJ is all about.

The Second Layer

In the second layer of the PAIJ we can dig deeper in the narrative of reversal and ask - why is this story so important for the culture? Although the answer is already evident, this second layer amplifies it even more. This is the section in which I introduce the timeline leading to 1844 and explore the meaning of the final judgment in the earthly sanctuary. In doing so, I introduce the centrality of Jesus both in the timeline and in the sanctuary ritual. The main objective at this juncture is to amplify the withness of God in the narrative of redemption and the flow of human history.

The following outline is the one I use to explore this second layer:

1. First, I focus on the 2300-day prophecy as an answer to the question, "How long?" In the first layer, we explored the thematic answer to this question meaning we looked at God's overall goal to reverse suffering and restore humanity to its Edenic other-centered state. In this layer, we add to the thematic view by focusing on its historical flow which places the message within the arc of the human story. How long will suffering and injustice continue unchecked? According to the vision, the beginning of the end is 1844 when the final phase of the redemption story began. I then explore the cleansing of the sanctuary as the "final phase" of the ritual narrative in the OT and explore the idea that God is right now engaged in his final act to restore the world. This amplifies the relevance of the doctrine by placing it in the flow of human time.

   One of the challenges I have had over the years when it comes to exploring 1844 is that people simply check out. It's boring and tedious. But what I have found is that when a person is already excited about the narrative explored in the first layer, the doctrine now means something to them and as a result exploring its timeline goes from a seemingly pointless exercise in biblical arithmetic to an exciting puzzle into the heart and work of God.

2. Nevertheless, I don't get hung up on the date itself. Instead, I make sure to refocus on the centrality of Jesus in the 70 weeks and also on his centrality through the totality of the 2300 years, especially in its conclusion. Jesus is the central theme all the way through and, during the judgment phase itself, he remains the absolute center. This is also a good time to revisit the narrative of salvation that was lost during the age of the church.

3. The centrality of Jesus is then the foundation for amplifying the "agents of reversal" motif in which it is via a relationship with Jesus - not a religion - that his other-centered love flows through us to a world increasingly lost in injustice, oppression and self-preservation. This idea is then further amplified by the apocalyptic theme of religio-political

oppression resurging in the final days of history.

The Third Layer

Finally, the third layer emerges as the most in depth exploration of the doctrine. In this phase, the student explores the place of the PAIJ in the continuum of Christian theology. Here they can learn how the Adventist approach to theology differs from other systems of thought and provides it with a deep logic on suffering and the reversal of suffering not only as a protest of religio-political injustice but as a cleansing of the very heart of the sinner from self-centered to other-centered love. This process is connected to the Hebrew ritual of "afflicting the soul" (also known as fasting) during Yom Kippur - not as a religio-centric and ascetic expression of faith but as an identification with the suffering that is perpetuated in the world via our own self-centered human will. This then results in an exploration of how our authentic self is part of the history of evil which God reverses in us and consequently, in the world around us.

We see this reality expressed best in Isaiah 58:1-12 in which the people of Israel ask, "'Why have we fasted,' they say, 'and you have not seen it? Why have we humbled ourselves, and you have not noticed?'"(3). God's answer through the rest of the chapter is that he rejects their soul-affliction because it has not led to the reversal of suffering and injustice in their communities. In other words, it is a phony and artificial affliction in which the Israelites fasted and did all the proper rituals and yet, their affliction was entirely disconnected from the alleviation and reversal of suffering. As a result, God rejects their affliction of soul as a synthetic forgery of the real thing. In other words, the Israelites were worshiping God while holding on to the impulse of self within. But in the day of Atonement, God was calling them to turn their eyes to the sacrifice and forsake the impulse of self entirely. Thus, God responds in Isaiah:

> "Is not this the kind of fasting I have chosen: to loose the chains of injustice and untie the cords of the yoke, to set the oppressed free and break every yoke? Is it not to share your food with the hungry and to provide the poor wanderer with shelter—when you see the naked, to clothe them, and not to turn away from your own flesh and blood? Then your light will break forth like the dawn, and your healing will quickly appear; then your righteousness will go before you..." (6-8)

It is clear from Isaiah then, that the purpose of afflicting the soul is not religious austerity but the reversal of suffering through the healing of self within resulting in the perpetuation of love to those around us. And yet, how often have I heard Adventist preachers speak of the PAIJ in a puritanistic fashion in which the objective is to hyper analyse one's life for sin? How often have these supposed champions of the straight testimony completely missed the mark by being absorbed in surface idiosyncrasies and minor lifestyle issues while ignoring the legitimate worries that surround us? In fact, I have heard some Adventist preachers argue that the reason we should not sing joyful worship songs in our churches is because we ought to be afflicting our souls during the antitypical day of atonement. Really? Is this what our message is all about? Why have I never heard these pious men sound a radical call to step out of our religious frugality and embrace the call to be agents of life, joy and redemption in our communities. Why have I not heard them rage against the systems of oppression in our society, against the institutional and systemic perpetuation of racial inequality, discrimination against minorities, refugees and migrants, poverty and the abuse of the vulnerable. The sad consequence in my experience, is entire generations of Adventists obsessively fixated on whether they have overcome their addiction to cheese or chocolate but with seemingly zero concern for the outcast, the distress of the LGBTIQ+ community or any of the real agonizing dramas that everyday people are navigating.

In this third layer, this call to affliction is emphasised once more alongside the centrality of Jesus in the narrative. This is key because the final cleansing ritual clearly has the sacrifice as the central theme (see Leviticus 16) demonstrating an extra emphasis on God's solution and not mans. Thus, while we are called to recognise our own place in the perpetuation of suffering and to actively work to reverse the suffering around us we are also called to focus on Jesus who alone can reverse the impulse of self within and restore us to the image of love.

Thus, this third layer is the phase in which I introduce students to the tensions between Calvinist and Arminian theology, amplify the call to active be agents of reversal and explore how the sanctuary and PAIJ interact with those tensions providing Adventism with a unique message otherwise unheard of. This then amplifies the importance of our end-time message not as a propaganda campaign for the Seventh-day Adventist institution (which our traditional frameworks often come across as) but as a call for God's people to abandon the systemic fabric of suffering and selfishness personified in the beast, the dragon and Babylon itself. Even the message on the mark of the beast becomes less about what day the Sabbath is and more about the narrative of humanitarian and ecological justice that undergirds the Sabbath. This reframes our end times message as a call for humanitarian justice and a protest against the perpetuation of religious intolerance and coercion as opposed to the tired arguments over "first day versus seventh-day".

The outline that I use for this third layer looks like this:

1. With a foundational understanding of the sanctuary and PAIJ I introduce students to the tensions between the Calvinist and Arminian approaches to scriptures salvation story. Now exploring this is way beyond the scope of this article series bit if you are interested in more, I recommend the article, "Why the Critics of the Investigative Judgment Failed" and also my books, "Weirdventism: Adventism for a Post-Church Generation" and "The Hole in Adventism: Making Total Sense of the Old & New Covenant" (links in the Appendix).

2. One of the focuses of the tension between Calvinist and Arminian theology is how we understand the relationship of God to the world and how that relationship differs in the above systems. Because Calvinism and Arminianism constitute the stories that protestants tell the world, Adventism emerges as a unique story that resolves the tensions between the two and thus, provides

the culture with a perspective that has meaning and value for contemporary tensions in the individual and collective human currency.

3. The end focus of it all comes back to the centrality of Jesus and his plan to reverse the systems of suffering, end the struggle between love and self and cleanse the hearts of his people from the impulse of self to the impulse of other-centered love. Once again, the sources I pointed out in step one explores each of these in depth.

A Call to Discipleship

Some may be wondering; how can I do all this in an evangelistic series or Bible study set? The simple answer is you don't. And the reason why some of us may be tempted to do so is because Adventists are fundamentally terrible at discipleship. Our approach to the spiritual life tends to revolve around dumping information on people and then leaving them to fend for themselves. But this reframe and layered approach to the PAIJ demands a completely different method. It demands a progressive step by step path to discovering the depth of the doctrine and this cannot be accomplished in an evangelistic sermon series or a seekers Bible study set. First of all, it's too much to take in. Second of all, a person doesn't need this level of theological depth to get baptised. But if our churches redesigned themselves around discipleship pathways in which baptism is the beginning and not the end of the journey then the slow journey toward grasping the three layers of the PAIJ would be no problem.

My approach is that once a person understands the first layer of the doctrine, they understand its important themes and, all things being equal, are ready to become members of the Seventh-day Adventist movement. From there, after baptism, a discipleship pathway that takes them deeper must form part of the local church's strategy for spiritual growth and can empower and equip new believers over time and in manageable chunks as opposed to a giant truck load of theology being dumped onto them. I propose this approach will provide more meaning, relevance, and applicatory power to our members, new and old.

A Call to Redesign

However, one more point must be made. If we are to reframe our conceptualisation of the PAIJ to speak meaning and life into the universal primary idea of suffering, we must also redesign the way our local churches operate.

The vast majority of local Adventist churches are completely disconnected from their communities and the suffering inherent in those communities. But this reframe calls us to redesign our churches to do more than preach sermons and run programs. Instead, it calls us to change our priorities and structures to facilitate the reversal of suffering in the communities in which we reside through a two-tiered approach of story-telling and active service. The story-telling portion emphasizes our need to communicate the Biblical narrative of God's heart to our communities in clear and relevant theological thought. The active service portion emphasizes our need to put our money where our mouth is and do something more than use those mouths. To borrow from Adventist pastor Shawn Brace, when designing a vision for our churches we ought not to ask where our church will be in 10 years. Instead, we should ask - where will our community be in 10 years because we are here?

Will there be less alcoholism? Less suicide? Less loneliness? Less poverty? Less despair? Will our church be a space of reversal for suffering in our community and preach a gospel that reverses the impulse of self in the human heart, thus perpetuating a culture of other-centeredness in our neighborhoods? It is useless to preach a message that says, "God is reversing the systems and perpetuation of suffering" and then sit on our pews week after week - completely disconnected and isolated from the suffering that surrounds us. This practical involvement in our communities must also be part of our discipleship process that equips members to not only have healthy theology but practical involvement in their cities and towns.

Psychologist and Holocaust survivor Victor Frankl once wrote that as society advances people increasingly find themselves with the "means to live but no meaning to live for." This perspective applies not only to society at large but to the church as well. As Adventism moved further away from its roots in disappointment, heartbreak and suffering it became an institution rich in means and yet, it appears that we too lost the meaning we were raised for. This vision must be recaptured if we wish to transcend our Laodicean state in which we rest in the safety of our structures, policies and resources (which make us "rich and increased with goods") while simultaneously leaving us "miserable, and poor, and blind and naked." (Revelation 3: 16-17, *KJV*) A reframing of our faith that celebrates the supremacy of Jesus and the call to practical impact in the spaces we occupy is the only way.

Conclusion

By reframing the PAIJ in a universal primary idea like suffering, simplifying its mechanics by separating its understanding into 3 layers of depth to be studied over time, and providing practical applicatory power - including redesigning our local churches to exemplify the reversal of suffering in their communities - we will sweep the world with a message so relevant and powerful that the pillars of Satan's empire of self with be shaken to the core. And this, I believe, is what the Seventh-day Adventist church was called to do.

In the final article I will address some key questions that this framework raises and conclude with some closing thoughts.

Chapter Summary

- Our current method of teaching the PAIJ is entirely too complex.

- In order to help students capture the meaning of the PAIJ a new approach to teaching the PAIJ must be utilized. This approach breaks the doctrines exploration down into three levels of increasing depth. New students only have to understand the first layer to be ready for baptism. The second and third layer can be taught over time as the person grows in the knowledge of scripture.

- The three layer approach is not simply educational. It also calls us to adopt discipleship pathways in our churches and to redesign our ministries and church structures to facilitate the accomplishment of our true mission – to be agents of reversal in our communities, preparing the culture for the arrival of Jesus.

Discussion Questions

1. How capable are you of teaching the entirety of the PAIJ to a new believer in a meaningful and succinct manner?

2. How do you feel about the three-layer approach to teaching the PAIJ? Do you see how it can benefit both students and the church by encouraging discipleship above theological cramming? Or do you think there are inherent problems with this approach? Share your thoughts.

3. What changes can your church begin making to become a relevant agent of social and collective transformation in your sphere of influence? What changes can you personally make to do the same?

6.

Final Thoughts on the Death and Rebirth of the Investigative Judgment

"You can tell something isn't right when all your heroes come in black and white."

—— John Mayer

In the previous five articles I have made a simple case for the death and rebirth of the Pre-Advent Investigative Judgment (PAIJ). Its death, I have contended, is not due to a flaw in the doctrine itself but to the way in which it has been constrained to a framework that no longer engages universal primary ideas. In addition, the old frameworks have proved to be too complicated and difficult to not only learn but apply. Thus, the doctrines rebirth is found in contextualizing its essence to a universal primary idea and simplifying its anatomy. Only then will the doctrine speak value to the human experience which naturally results in applicatory power. The combination of these three simple elements will give the doctrine a renewed energy, relevance and identity.

However, several questions remain that need to be answered before we can close the series off. Thus, in this final article I will address five key questions that need to be understood before the reframe is complete.

Can't we develop a theology of "reversal of suffering" without the PAIJ?

The short answer is yes, and others have done so. The Radical Reformation is known for its emphasis on themes like justice, equity and mercy as well as its rejection of religio-political empires in favor of the kingdom of heaven motif. We also have the impact of Martin Luther King Jr. who understood the role of the gospel and the church was not merely to preach about a world to come, but to invest in reversing the sufferings perpetuated in this world. Contemporary evangelicals Tim Keller, Matthew Chandler and Jefferson Bethke understand the same. Classical Protestants like Dietrich Bonhoeffer and William and Catherine Booth (founders of the Salvation Army) all shared the same vision. Likewise, a theology of "reversal of suffering" can be derived from scripture by studying the love of God, the minor prophets and their call for justice (especially for widows, migrants and orphans), and the gospels. So then, what is the point of framing the PAIJ in suffering?

To answer this question, I will pose another question: What is the point of doctrine? Do individual doctrines exist to give us independently novel ideas and insights? Or do each of them exist as part of a narrative, to connect to the others and amplify scriptures main theme of God's love? If you believe the former, then you are likely to fall for the novelty fallacy - the idea that a doctrine must say something unheard of in order to have value. But if you believe the latter, then it is clear that doctrine doesn't have to say something unheard of elsewhere in scripture but has value in simply amplifying the narrative and driving us deeper into the love of God.

Adventists need to get over this obsession with having to be the only people on earth saying something no one else is saying. God didn't call us to be odd for the sake of being odd. Our movement is an outflow of the reformation, not some *sui generis* tribe. For those looking to be part of a church that communicates a narrative that is as uncommon as it is isolated, I recommend either the Roman Catholic Church, Jehovah's Witness or Latter-Day Saints. But for those looking for a church that, while not proclaiming some unusual message is nevertheless telling a unique and cohesive story that harmonizes all the beautiful elements of scripture into one seamless story - I give you Adventism.

Seriously, if we take an honest look at the sanctuary, we will find that there is nothing there that can't be derived from elsewhere in scripture. Justification can be derived without it. Sanctification can also be derived without it as well as glorification. The Great Controversy theme was first introduced by the reformer Jacobus Arminius and later expanded by John Wesley in what he referred to as scriptures "aesthetic theme". Neither of them had a doctrine of the sanctuary to drive their discovery. The doctrine of judgment (including both the righteous and the wicked) can also be found without the sanctuary and forms a core part of Arminian and Wesleyan soteriology. And themes like the high priestly ministry of Jesus are also easy to find outside of the PAIJ's framework. Therefore, there is nothing truly original or unique that Adventism possesses because of the sanctuary doctrine. Some might say 1844 is, but 1844 is an apocalyptic timeline that connects to the sanctuary and gives it contemporary and eschatological significance. It is not the sanctuary in itself.

Nevertheless, the sanctuary is extremely valuable. While this is beyond the scope of this article (See my books "Weirdvolution: Adventism for a Post-Church

Generation" and "The Hole in Adventism: Making Total Sense of the Old & New Covenant" for a deeper exploration - links in the Appendix) the key to the sanctuary is not that it gives us novel theological ideas but that it strings together the entire narrative of scripture into one cohesive and compelling worldview that is unheard of in Christian theology (in a unified sense). It is like a hub that connects all doctrines to the central theme of God's love and *withness* and in doing so, amplifies their significance and impact on the human story. The biblical theme of reversing suffering and standing for justice is one of those. The theme can be derived without the sanctuary, but with it the theme gains greater significance as it is tied to the heart of God and the apocalyptic perspective of societies endgame.

This reality becomes more significant when we realise that, despite the many great voices within Christian history who have called for justice and the reversal of suffering - the Christian church is still by and large disconnected from the theme of justice. In fact, the only reason why so many Christians talk about justice today is not because the church has led the way in the pursuit of reversing suffering but because secular pop-culture has made the pursuit of justice trendy. The church itself has, once again, come in at the tail end of the conversation and not the head.

But if we understand the significance of the sanctuary in the struggle over good and evil and the reversal of human empire and its collateral suffering then we have a vision for reversal that is deeper than "God is nice and we should be too". Instead, we have the theme of reversal deeply embedded into the thing that unifies all of scripture into one cohesive narrative - the sanctuary - providing us not simply with a nice idea but with a theme that has historical, soteriological, theodical and eschatological significance. And this, I would venture to say, is a vision of reversal that no other theological system has been able to match.

Take for example the Sabbath. Adventists are not the only ones who believe this. Neither are we the only ones who believe in the mortal soul, annihilationism (as opposed to eternal conscious torment in hell) and the "back to Eden" motif that undergirds our health message. These beliefs are shared randomly throughout Christendom. The same can be said for the theme of justice and the reversal of suffering. However, there is not one theological system that strings these together into one cohesive narrative. Instead, these concepts float around the marketplace of theological ideas with no actual place to call home. But in the sanctuary, the various themes that celebrate God's heart are drafted into one unified story. The Sabbath is thus connected to God's love, character, the gospel, the nature of man and the back to Eden motif. In addition, through the sanctuary the Sabbath is connected to eschatology and thus leaps forth with significantly more meaning for Adventists than what the Seventh Day Baptists, without a sanctuary vision, have been able to communicate. It is this ability to string the call to be agents of reversal throughout the entirety of the scriptural narrative - including its eschatological elements - that makes the sanctuary so central to its development.

Think of it this way. While we can derive a vision of justice and reversal of suffering throughout all of scripture, the sanctuary connects these ideas to the Great Controversy undergirding the visions in Daniel. Thus, we see that part of God's call to reverse suffering includes the epilogue of the struggle between good and evil. But it goes further. Daniel also depicts the end of human empire. Thus, the sanctuary finds itself at the center of the battle between human and divine governments. Human empire is deconstructed and demolished as part of the reversal of suffering that brings the universe back to harmony and concludes the atonement in its entirety. But it goes deeper than that. The sanctuary doesn't simply connect to the end of the Great Controversy and the end of human empire. It also connects to the end of the beastly impulse of self that drives every human heart. Thus, in the sanctuary we find, not simply a call to reverse the suffering caused by satanic and human empire, but to reverse the suffering caused by our own impulse for self-preservation. This can only be accomplished by the gospel thus placing the centrality of Jesus front and center without falling into the antinomian trap of sweeping injustice under the rug in the name of grace. The sanctuary thus points us to Jesus as our only hope but also calls us, in light of his grace, to open our hearts to be healed from self to love so that the reversal of suffering in this world begins with us, then moves onto empire and finally the complete eradication of Satan's government highlighted by the scapegoat ritual.

So, the short answer is yes, we can derive a reversal of suffering motif from elsewhere in scripture, but that doesn't take away from the fact that the PAIJ emphasizes and amplifies that motif in multicolor. As a result, the call to be agents of reversal transcends a mere concept in scripture and becomes a part of the church's identity in the last days both through the reversal of the impulse of self in the human heart and the reversal of suffering in our communities. As these two realities coalesce the church then gains the rapport necessary to effectively proclaim the coming of a new kingdom which will bring a complete end to not only human empire, but to the very government of self. The invitation to be part of that kingdom is thus extended to all who receive Christ by faith - an experience that migrates the soul from a citizen of selfishness to a citizen of agape love. All of these concepts are bolstered by the deep logic for reversal provided by an apocalyptic doctrine like the PAIJ.

How does reframing the PAIJ in suffering interact with the doctrine's historic priorities?

The doctrines historic priorities are:
1. The sanctuary in heaven is being cleansed from the record of sin
2. The cleansing is symbolic of judgment, which began with the church as a process in 1844
3. When the cleansing of the sanctuary is complete, Jesus will return to gather his people

The reframes priorities are:

1. The sanctuary represents God's connection with man that is being restored at the end of time
2. The restoration of the sanctuary is the beginning of the end of separation and suffering
3. While God reverses the separation and the suffering, he commissions his people to be agents of reversal in the world until he returns with his new kingdom

While the reframe is certainly different, recall from the previous chapter that its purpose is not to replace or undo the historic priorities of the PAIJ. In the second and third layers of exploration, those historic priorities reemerge and in fact, find an even greater level of depth and meaning when seen through the lens of the reframe. Thus, the purpose of the reframe as seen above is to introduce and explain the doctrine in connection with a universal primary idea that the culture finds relevant. Once that connection has been made, other elements of the doctrine that a person would previously have considered pointless gain a greater sense of meaning and value.

Does this reframe somehow damage our apocalyptic warning to the world?

Our apocalyptic warning in light of the PAIJ is that we are in the final phase of the salvation story and there's no time to play around.

The new framework holds the same warning. We don't have time to get comfortable with the systems that perpetuate suffering. The gospel must be preached. Suffering must be reversed. And those who claim to be Christians while holding on to the impulse of self and allying themselves to the systems and structures that perpetuate suffering in this world (be they political, ideological or religious) will not see the kingdom of heaven. This is the final phase of the story of redemption and if ever there was an urgent time to make up our minds as to which kingdom we belong to, this is it.

The importance of this perspective cannot be underestimated. During a recent basketball game at one of our Adventist universities an anonymous student began a repulsive racist commentary on social media against the black players. When the student was confronted with God's judgment over such things, the response was, "I am washed in the blood of Jesus. I will not come into judgment."

The PAIJ says "think again."

When John Earnest walked into a California Synagogue on April 27, 2019 and opened fire killing one and injuring three, few people knew he was a committed member of a Presbyterian church who, in his manifesto, articulated the gospel beautifully when he wrote, "I did not choose to be a Christian. The Father chose me. The Son saved me. And the Spirit keeps me."[1] Earnest later added, "Know that you are saved in Christ and nothing—not death, nor torture, nor sin—can steal your soul away from God."[2]

The PAIJ says, "not so fast".

It's not enough to simply preach the good news of forgiveness and assurance of salvation. It's also not enough to emphasise the one-dimensional sanctification Adventists are so fond of in which all our focus is placed on God helping us overcome our personal sins with hardly a word on how the gospel transforms us into defenders of the marginalized, protectors of the vulnerable, voices for the voiceless and deliverers of the oppressed. No wonder emerging generations of Adventist youth find the church so irrelevant. Our members go on about the evils of seemingly insignificant things like coffee but remain silent on issues that truly perpetuate suffering and injustice in the world.

Something must change. We must preach the good news of salvation, the beauty of assurance in the finished work of Jesus to which we add no merit but we must also capture a meaningful vision of individual regeneration - not the cheesy obsession with personal piety but a belief in the work of the Holy Spirit to reverse the impulse of self in the human heart and restore it to divine love. Jemar Tisby said it best when he wrote that many pastors "view of the gospel only focuses on issues of personal salvation and individual piety. It never touches broader matters of systemic and institutional injustice."[3] This must change and I propose that the PAIJ provides Adventism with the raw materials needed for us to lead the way in this sphere of truth especially as we approach the apocalyptic setting in which selfishness and injustice will rise to its apex of power in its final act of rebellion against God.

Why didn't Ellen White teach this reframe? Isn't what she taught all that we should teach?

The idea that if Ellen White didn't say it then neither should we is a flawed perspective on a number of levels. First of all, Seventh-day Adventists are a people of one book - the Bible. Ellen White's entire ministry was devoted to calling us back to the Bible. To suggest that a perspective is wrong simply because it goes beyond what Ellen White said is to place Ellen White above the Bible and, in a sense, make her no different to the Pope who has the final say on theological matters within the Roman church.

But of course, the idea itself contradicts Ellen White's own belief system. Here are a few quotes that can help us see that building on what Ellen White and the pioneers left us is not only theologically sound, it is theologically required:

> Whenever the people of God are growing in grace, they will be constantly obtaining a clearer understanding of His word. They will discern new light and beauty in its sacred

truths. This has been true in the history of the church in all ages, and thus it will continue to the end. But as real spiritual life declines, it has ever been the tendency to cease to advance in the knowledge of the truth. Men rest satisfied with the light already received from God's word, and discourage any further investigation of the Scriptures. They become conservative, and seek to avoid discussion.[4]

We must not think, "Well, we have all the truth, we understand the main pillars of our faith, and we may rest on this knowledge." The truth is an advancing truth, and we must walk in the increasing light.[5]

There is no excuse for anyone in taking the position that there is no more truth to be revealed, and that all our expositions of Scripture are without an error. The fact that certain doctrines have been held as truth for many years by our people, is not a proof that our ideas are infallible. Age will not make error into truth, and truth can afford to be fair. No true doctrine will lose anything by close investigation.[6]

A spirit of pharisaism has been coming in upon the people who claim to believe the truth for these last days. They are self-satisfied. They have said, "We have the truth. There is no more light for the people of God." But we are not safe when we take a position that we will not accept anything else than that upon which we have settled as truth.... Our minds have become so narrow that we do not seem to understand that the Lord has a mighty work to do for us. Increasing light is to shine upon us...[7]

Of course, the above quotes do not mean Ellen White endorsed the idea that we would someday discover we were completely wrong and have to abandon our pillars for entirely new foundations. She was adamant throughout her ministry that our pillars are sound. Rather, her point is that we ought to build on them and not settle for what we have learned in the past. The landmarks give us the raw materials to construct meaningful perspectives as time and culture ebbs and flows. We should not stay locked in outdated frameworks in the name of "faithfulness." To the contrary, such an attitude demonstrates a spirit contrary to the truth, not for it.

Nevertheless, the idea that the PAIJ can be reframed in suffering and understood as a call for the reversal of the impulse of self that perpetuates suffering and injustice in the world, while not explicitly worded this way in Whites writings, is nevertheless compatible with her overall message. For example:

> The atonement of Christ is not a mere skillful way to have our sins pardoned; it is a divine remedy for the cure of transgression and the restoration of spiritual health. It is the Heaven-ordained means by which the righteousness of Christ may be not only upon us but in our hearts and characters.[8]

> In cleansing the temple from the world's buyers and sellers, Jesus announced His mission to cleanse the heart from the defilement of sin, — from the earthly desires, the selfish lusts, the evil habits, that corrupt the soul.[9]

> While the investigative judgment is going forward in Heaven, while the sins of penitent believers are being removed from the sanctuary, there is to be a special work of purification, of putting away of sin, among God's people upon earth.[10]

Sadly, the history of Adventism is replete with a misuse of these statements of Ellen White. They have been used to promote a legalistic, often fanatical, rules-obsessed religion that undermines the beauty of Christs centrality and supremacy in our salvation story. But when viewed from the perspective of becoming agents of reversal in our communities, the statements take on and entirely new tone. Rather than being a call to ultra-conservative, somber religion they are a call to something entirely other centered - an invitation to forsake the impulse of self and allow God's grace to remake us in the image of agape love. The end result of such an experience is a community of people who live with the goal of reversing the suffering that surrounds them. I couldn't think of anything more awesome to do with my life than this.

If this framework emphasizes the experiential over the legal aspect of the gospel, how does it avoid the trap of legalism?

Historically, the Adventist church has been plagued by theological paradigms that emphasise works over grace, "do's" over *done,* and sanctification over justification. The end result has been systems of thought such as Last Generation Theology where grace, while never denied, is practically suppressed. In the more liberal side of the equation, an emphasis on social justice or the social gospel has also been placed over Jesus' substitutionary atonement to the point that its centrality is lost.

However, in the present framework the objective is not human works, either from the conservative obsession with personal piety or the liberal preoccupation with political activism. Rather the objective is the liberation of the heart from selfishness to love. This liberation cannot be accomplished by anything other than Jesus-only.

Our assurance remains rooted in his substitutionary atonement alone. Nevertheless, this atonement envisions more than legal pardon but the actual healing of the human heart from a host for selfishness and the perpetuation of suffering to a host for other centeredness and the reversal of suffering. A gospel that promises pardon while accommodating the impulse of self that leads to suffering in our circles of influence is no gospel at all. And yet, to think that social involvement can somehow earn us salvation is a ridiculous notion. We are not saved by reversing suffering, we reverse suffering because we have been saved from the dominion of self to begin with. The natural outcome of anyone who has entered into life is to become a propagator of that life in all its abundance.

So, the short answer is, the framework from suffering does not emphasise the experiential aspects of the gospel in the same way conservatives and liberals tend to do. Rather, it emphasizes the condition of the human heart which can only be healed through grace. This then results naturally in a life that lives in harmony with the universal design of agape love.

The trap of legalism is thus avoided by rejecting the presuppositions that lead to legalism. Jesus-only remains the center of the narrative. Grace is never subverted to works but is rather elevated as the only real solution to the condition of the human heart. And that same grace then flows through us to others in selfless living. The failure of systems like Last Generation Theology is that they subvert grace to works, overemphasize personal piety and, to a large degree, are driven by Eurocentric value structures in which holiness is viewed primarily through the lens of white culture. In my experience, this system of thought perpetuates suffering wherever it is fully embraced. Likewise, liberals who emphasise works over grace tend to lean toward the cause of social justice and see themselves not merely as agents of reversal in suffering but as crusaders against empire. This leads many to make a gospel out of activism and political involvement when the gospel is about transforming human hearts, not institutions or systems. Should we combat institutions and systems of oppression whenever possible? Yes! But we must never forget that the gospel is greater because it promises not just the undoing of unjust policies but the transformation of the hearts that immortalize those unjust policies - your heart and mine.

Thus, while Daniel and Revelation reveal that we are to rage against the systems of suffering God alone will destroy empire. Our work is not to be on the offensive against empire through an imbalanced commitment to legislative measures or the like, but to focus on building the alternate kingdom of God through the church. When Jesus returns, he will take care of empire himself as envisioned in the book of Revelation.

The emphasis is therefore clear - what we need more of in this world is Jesus. Not more Adventism. Not more religion. Not more rules. Not more theology. And certainly not more works. We need more Jesus - a Jesus who forgives, transforms and releases us into the suffering to point the world to the one who will bring about its ultimate and utter annihilation.

Can you explain how this perspective differs from Last Generation Theology more? Isn't LGT all about how we must vindicate God? Aren't you saying that by being agents of reversal we vindicate God? How is this any different?

There is a link to a series of articles I wrote titled, "The Unbearable Failure of Last Generation Theology" in the Appendix that goes into more detail. For now, allow me to briefly expand my case. The problem with LGT is not that it has a vindication of God motif. Its problem is how it frames it. Without dissecting the system of thought too much (beyond the scope of this article) allow me to make three brief observations in addition to the ones made above.

1. Unlike most who say the fault with LGT is in how it defines sin (sin as willful choice instead of sin as nature) I propose that the true fault with LGT is that it is built on a faulty understanding of the law. Instead of seeing God's law as the design for life flowing from his heart of love, LGT leans toward seeing the law of God as a set of rules God imposes on humanity. In other words, LGT sees God, Christianity, and holiness primarily through the lens of legal compliance. (You must do x, y and z or else...) By viewing the law as a legal code, we must comply with, LGT paints a picture of a tyrannical God demanding perfect compliance from his human subjects. This leads to an unhealthy and tragic religious experience.

    It is from this imposed law construct that LGT derives its meaning of sin as willful choice. Thus, when debating the nature of sin, LGT proponents will often quote 1 John 3:4 "sin is the transgression of the law" (*KJV*) as evidence that sin is a willful act of breaking the law. However, what I have never seen them do is go further and ask *what exactly is the law?* If the law is a legally imposed demand, then it makes sense that sin is a willful choice to transgress that legal demand. But if the law is the design of reality and based on Gods heart of love then the transgression of the law is synonymous with the transgression of love. From there we have to ask, "why are human beings 'love-breakers'?" To say, "we break love willfully" begs the question, "why?" to which sin as a state of being, nature or character emerge as the only possible solutions. Thus, if we reject the legally imposed perspective on the law, LGT loses its plausibility as a legitimate perspective on scriptures narrative.

2. The other element to change from a "law is love" perspective is our understanding of perfection. Perfection is no longer a legal demand but an experience of healing. It goes from being a tyrannical and unfair concept to a romantic and beautiful experience to pursue because rather than pursuing perfect compliance to a list of rules we find ourselves longing for perfect harmony with love. And as

we long for our lives to be in perfect harmony with love, we naturally become more loving, more kind, more merciful, more inclusive, more inspiring and - in turn - agents of reversal in a world steeped in suffering perpetuated by the impulse of self.

3. Finally, we arrive at vindication. With a "law is love" motif, vindication takes on a whole new meaning. In this view, we understand that the vindication of God has two separate elements to it. I personally refer to these two elements as ontological vs pragmatic vindication.

    Ontological vindication is what Jesus did. Because Jesus vindicated God at the cross, the great controversy is over in a cosmic sense. There is no more doubt among the unfallen that God is love and Satan is a liar. All the charges have been answered. If humanity never accepted the sacrifice and went on in rebellion God could eventually judge and annihilate the entire planet without raising any questions before the universe as to his goodness. It was all answered in Jesus at the cross. LGT on the other hand, teaches that the GC cannot end until a final generation becomes perfect. And if they don't then God loses the GC. So, it makes the end of the GC contingent on humans and thus, the final generation becomes a type of co-redeemer with Christ. Jesus didn't fully vindicate God at the cross, so humans now have to become perfect in order to show that God's law is fair, and the gospel works. However, the gospel assures us that the main struggle in the GC (God's heart) has been resolved in Christ. Man is not needed to add to that in any cosmic sense. That's ontological vindication.

By pragmatic vindication, what is meant is that, unlike the unfallen who can see the drama play out mostly from the outside, humans are caught on the inside of the struggle. Jesus' vindication on the cross then, while complete, remains unknown to us unless it is communicated to us. And God has chosen that that communication will take place via the church. But if the church is a perpetuator of injustice and suffering (rooted in lies about God), then the vindication never happens. So, the church must embrace the call to be reversers of injustice and suffering as well as lies about God. In doing so, we take the finished vindication of God in Christ and present it pragmatically to the world. God doesn't need us to end the GC but he's not in this to win some PR campaign. He genuinely wants to save people because he loves them. So, he waits. And as the church lives out that character of God pragmatically (that is in tangible, practical ways) his ontological vindication spreads throughout the world, melts hardened hearts, and brings more people into a trusting relationship with him. That's pragmatic vindication.

Because LGT sees the law as a legal demand, it sees sin as willful choice and in turn, it sees holiness and perfection of character as willful choice as well. Anyone who fails does so because they are not willfully choosing to be holy and perfect, or to trust in God enough, or to be serious enough in their faith. Delete the legal law view, and all of this fades away. A "law is love" vision sees sin as a condition of love-lessness which the gospel heals. When we receive Jesus this process of reversal of love-lessness or the reversal of the impulse of self in the human heart, begins. This process is a healing process that takes a person's entire life. But as we walk with God and allow him to heal our selfishness, we naturally become agents of reversal in the world. As a result, our characters are perfected and God's name is vindicated pragmatically, not because of anything we are doing, but because of the work God is doing in us and through us. And when the judgment ends, there will be two people left on the earth - those who clung to the impulse of self within and those who, weak and broken as they might be, trusted God to heal them from self to love. And it is those, justified by his love and sanctified in his love who will be glorified by and in and to his love to dwell in a kingdom and a universe in which love-only reigns supreme. Ellen White put it best at the conclusion of *The Great Controversy* when she wrote,

> One pulse of harmony and gladness beats through the vast creation. From Him who created all, flow life and light and gladness, throughout the realms of illimitable space. From the minutest atom to the greatest world, all things, animate and inanimate, in their unshadowed beauty and perfect joy, declare that God is love.[11]

Conclusion

While I am certain many more questions will emerge over time, I would like to conclude this series with a brief summary of its main contention. In his song "Speak for Me", musician John Mayer laments the state of modernity when he sings, "something isn't right when all your heroes come in black and white." The poem can be understood in two ways. First, that something is wrong with modernity in that is has no contemporary heroes and thus, the one looking for a hero must turn to the past. Or second, that something is wrong with modernity in that it is blind to its own heroes. In other words, it is so nostalgically obsessed with a bygone generation that it is missing out on the possibilities before it.

If we take the second interpretation, I would contend that this is a problem for Adventism today. We appear to be nostalgic about what was to the detriment of what can be. And the results of this wistful sentiment are before us, easy to observe if we open our eyes. But the good news is, it's not too late.

In the past six articles I have not attempted to defend the historic or theological validity of the PAIJ. Undoubtedly, many who reject its historic and theological validity will likewise reject this entire series and that is okay. I have no intention of proving them otherwise. My objective in this series has been simple: to explore, not the doctrines validity (which is addressed in multiple other sources), but its utility. By reframing, simplifying and applying it, it is my hope that every reader has been challenged and inspired with a new vision for the PAIJ that has also redefined their vision of church and faith as a whole. Even if you found yourself disagreeing with particular points - or perhaps with my entire framework - I hope you at least embrace the call to reframe the PAIJ to the universal primary ideas that your context is immersed in.

To the end of time my hope is that the Adventist movement would capture its true calling as a voice for the suffering with a story of God's heart unheard of in our world. May we flood the culture with this radical and overwhelming narrative until that day when we see the one in whom all our hopes and desires reside.

Chapter Summary

- A number of common questions and concerns were explored including how this reframe relates to and interacts with the PAIJ's historic priorities.

- Reframing the PAIJ does not dilute our message to the culture. To the contrary, our message is already diluted because no one pays attention to it or finds any meaning in it. A reframe is counter-intuitive because while it evolves the doctrine, it is also the thing which makes it capable of fulfilling its mission as a practical, life-changing idea.

- Regardless of whether you have found the present reframe compelling or not, the truth remains that our historic framework does not connect with anyone who is not already an Adventist (rare exceptions omitted). A new approach – or more likely, a diversity of new approaches – must be nurtured in order for our message to have the impact we intend for it to have.

Discussion Questions

1. What questions, concerns or struggles would you ask regarding the suggested reframe in this book?

2. How would you improve on, or adapt the present reframe to be more effective and meaningful at speaking value to contemporary, post-church culture?

3. What changes do you feel inspired to pursue in your life and local church after reading this book? What is the first step you will take toward implementing those changes?

Chapter Endnotes

1. Relevant Magazine. "Alleged Synagogue Shooter Proclaims Christianity, Evangelical Pastors Struggle to Understand," [Web: https://relevantmagazine.com/current/alleged-synagogue-shooter-proclaims-christianity-evangelical-pastors-struggle-to-understand]

2. Hukabee, Tyler. "Will the Evangelical Church Reckon with Its Terrorists?" [Web: https://relevantmagazine.com/god/church/will-the-evangelical-church-reckon-with-its-terrorists]

3. Tisby, Jemar. "Why white nationalism tempts white Christians," [Web: https://religionnews.com/2019/05/01/why-white-nationalism-tempts-white-christians]

4. White, Ellen G. "Counsels to Writers and Editors," p. 38.

5. *ibid.*, p. 33

6. *ibid.*, p. 35

7. White, Ellen G. *The Review and Herald*, June 18, 1889

8. White, Ellen G. *Biblical Commentary,* (vol. 6) p. 1074

9. White, Ellen G. "The Desire of Ages," p. 161

10. White, Ellen G. "The Great Controversy," p. 425

11. *ibid.*, p. 678

Appendix

Books for Further Reading

Weirdvolution: Adventism for a Post-Church Generation

The Hole in Adventism: Making Total Sense of the Old and New Covenant

Articles for Further Reading

Why the Critics of the Investigative Judgment Have Failed

The Unbearable Failure of Last Generation Theology (p1)

The Unbearable Failure of Last Generation Theology (p2)

The Unbearable Failure of Last Generation Theology (p3)

If you enjoyed this book...

If you enjoyed this book then I have good news for you. At the moment, I am in the process of writing an entire book on all of Daniel. In this new book I approach the book of Daniel from a totally different perspective with the aim of mining relevance and meaning from the text for emerging Millennial, Zed – and overall – post-church generations.

This new book will come in both electronic and print format and I hope to have it all done by the end of the year. To be among the first to know when it's released, join my Newsletter at:

thestorychurchproject.com/start

Once you subscribe you will receive a free copy of my eBook "*How to Study the Bible With Postmoderns*" so make sure you check your inbox!

Pastor Marcos Torres is a millennial Adventist pastor with a passion for reaching postmoderns and secular culture with the story of Jesus. He currently pastors in Western Australia where he lives with his wife and two children. He is also the host of *The Story Church Project*: a digital ministry focused on redesigning local Adventist churches for mission.

You can follow his project at:
thestorychurchproject.com

www.ingramcontent.com/pod-product-compliance
Lightning Source LLC
Chambersburg PA
CBHW032120040426
42449CB00005B/200